GW00602804

Llewellyn's

Witches' Datebook

2001

Featuring

Art by Kathleen Edwards. Text by Estelle Daniels, Gerina
Dunwich, Marguerite Elsbeth, Breid Foxsong, Yasmine
Galenorn, Magenta Griffith, Lady Gyngere of the Grove,
Kirin Lee, Edain McCoy, Dorothy Morrison, Ann
Moura, Steven Posch, and Jami Shoemaker

ISBN 1-56718-969-5

2001

JANUARY	FEBRUARY	MARCH	APRIL
S M T W T F S	S M T W T F S	S M T W T F S	S M T W T F S
1 2 3 4 5 6	1 2 3	1 2 3	1 2 3 4 5 6 7
7 8 9 10 11 12 13	4 5 6 7 8 9 10	4 5 6 7 8 9 10	8 9 10 11 12 13 14
14 15 16 17 18 19 20	11 12 13 14 15 16 17	11 12 13 14 15 16 17	15 16 17 18 19 20 21
21 22 23 24 25 26 27	18 19 20 21 22 23 24	18 19 20 21 22 23 24	22 23 24 25 26 27 28
28 29 30 31	25 26 27 28	25 26 27 28 29 30 31	29 30

MAY	JUNE	JULY	AUGUST
S M T W T F S	S M T W T F S	S M T W T F S	S M T W T F S
1 2 3 4 5	1 2	1 2 3 4 5 6 7	1 2 3 4
6 7 8 9 10 11 12	3 4 5 6 7 8 9	8 9 10 11 12 13 14	5 6 7 8 9 10 11
13 14 15 16 17 18 19	10 11 12 13 14 15 16	15 16 17 18 19 20 21	12 13 14 15 16 17 18
20 21 22 23 24 25 26	17 18 19 20 21 22 23	22 23 24 25 26 27 28	19 20 21 22 23 24 25
27 28 29 30 31	24 25 26 27 28 29 30	29 30 31	26 27 28 29 30 31

SEPTEMBER	OCTOBER	NOVEMBER	DECEMBER
S M T W T F S	S M T W T F S	S M T W T F S	S M T W T F S
1	1 2 3 4 5 6	1 2 3	1
2 3 4 5 6 7 8	7 8 9 10 11 12 13	4 5 6 7 8 9 10	2 3 4 5 6 7 8
9 10 11 12 13 14 15	14 15 16 17 18 19 20	11 12 13 14 15 16 17	9 10 11 12 13 14 15
16 17 18 19 20 21 22	21 22 23 24 25 26 27	18 19 20 21 22 23 24	16 17 18 19 20 21 22
23 24 25 26 27 28 29	28 29 30 31	25 26 27 28 29 30	23 24 25 26 27 28 29
30			30 31

2002

JANUARY	FEBRUARY	MARCH	APRIL
S M T W T F S	S M T W T F S	S M T W T F S	S M T W T F S
1 2 3 4 5	1 2	1 2	1 2 3 4 5 6
6 7 8 9 10 11 12	3 4 5 6 7 8 9	3 4 5 6 7 8 9	7 8 9 10 11 12 13
13 14 15 16 17 18 19	10 11 12 13 14 15 16	10 11 12 13 14 15 16	14 15 16 17 18 19 20
20 21 22 23 24 25 26	17 18 19 20 21 22 23	17 18 19 20 21 22 23	21 22 23 24 25 26 27
27 28 29 30 31	24 25 26 27 28	24 25 26 27 28 29 30	28 29 30
		31	

MAY	JUNE	JULY	AUGUST
S M T W T F S	S M T W T F S	S M T W T F S	S M T W T F S
1 2 3 4	1	1 2 3 4 5 6	1 2 3
5 6 7 8 9 10 11	2 3 4 5 6 7 8	7 8 9 10 11 12 13	4 5 6 7 8 9 10
12 13 14 15 16 17 18	9 10 11 12 13 14 15	14 15 16 17 18 19 20	11 12 13 14 15 16 17
19 20 21 22 23 24 25	16 17 18 19 20 21 22	21 22 23 24 25 26 27	18 19 20 21 22 23 24
26 27 28 29 30 31	23 24 25 26 27 28 29	28 29 30 31	25 26 27 28 29 30 31
	30		

SEPTEMBER	OCTOBER	NOVEMBER	DECEMBER
S M T W T F S	S M T W T F S	S M T W T F S	S M T W T F S
1 2 3 4 5 6 7	1 2 3 4 5	1 2	1 2 3 4 5 6 7
8 9 10 11 12 13 14	6 7 8 9 10 11 12	3 4 5 6 7 8 9	8 9 10 11 12 13 14
15 16 17 18 19 20 21	13 14 15 16 17 18 19	10 11 12 13 14 15 16	15 16 17 18 19 20 21
22 23 24 25 26 27 28	20 21 22 23 24 25 26	17 18 19 20 21 22 23	22 23 24 25 26 27 28
29 30	27 28 29 30 31	24 25 26 27 28 29 30	29 30 31

Editing/design by K. M. Brielmaier and Sharon Leah

Cover illustration and interior art © 2000 by Kathleen Edwards

Cover design and coloring by Anne-Marie Garrison

Art direction by Lynne Menturweck

Moon sign and phase data by Astro Communications Services

Table of Contents

How to Use Llewellyn's Witches' Datebook

W elcome to *Llewellyn's Witches' Datebook 2001*. This datebook was designed especially for Witches, Pagans, and magical people. Use it to plan sabbat celebrations, magic, Full Moon rites, and even dentist appointments! Below is a symbol key to some of the features of this datebook. In addition, *there is a symbol key on the inside back cover flap of this book* that you can leave open next to the book for easy reference.

MOON QUARTERS: The Moon's cycle is divided into four quarters, which are noted in the calendar pages along with their exact times. When the Moon changes quarter, both quarters are listed, as well as the time of the change. In addition, a symbol for the new quarter is placed where the numeral for the date usually appears.

MOON IN THE SIGNS: Approximately every two-and-a-half days the Moon moves from one zodiac sign to the next. The sign that the Moon is in at the beginning of the day (midnight Eastern Standard Time) is noted next to the quarter listing. If the Moon changes signs that day, there will be a notation saying "☽ enters" followed by the symbol for the sign it is entering.

MOON VOID-OF-COURSE: Just before the Moon enters a new sign it will make one final aspect (angular relationship) to another planet. Between that last aspect and the entrance of the Moon into the next sign it is said to be void-of-course. Activities begun when the Moon is void rarely come to fruition, or they turn out very differently than planned.

PLANETARY MOVEMENT: When a planet or asteroid moves from one sign into another, this change (called an *ingress*) is noted on the calendar pages with the exact time. The Moon and Sun are considered planets in this case. The planets (except for the Sun and Moon) can also appear to move backward as seen from the Earth. This is called a *planetary retrograde*, and is noted on the calendar pages with the symbol ℞. When the planet begins to move forward, or direct, again, it is marked D, and the time is also noted.

PLANTING AND HARVESTING DAYS: The best days for planting and harvesting are noted on the calendar pages with a seedling icon (planting) and a scythe icon (harvesting).

TIME ZONE CHANGES: The times and dates of all astrological phenomena in this datebook are based on Eastern Standard Time (EST). If you live outside of EST, you will need to make the following changes: Pacific Standard Time (PST) subtract three hours; Mountain Standard Time (MST) subtract two hours; Central Standard Time (CST) subtract one hour; Alaska/Hawaii subtract five hours; and during Daylight Saving Time add an hour.

Planets

☉	Sun	♆	Neptune
☽	Moon	♇	Pluto
☿	Mercury	⚷	Chiron
♀	Venus	⚳	Ceres
♂	Mars	⚴	Pallas
♃	Jupiter	⚵	Juno
♄	Saturn	⚶	Vesta
♅	Uranus		

Signs

♈	Aries	♐	Sagittarius
♉	Taurus	♑	Capricorn
♊	Gemini	♒	Aquarius
♋	Cancer	♓	Pisces
♌	Leo		
♍	Virgo		
♎	Libra		
♏	Scorpio		

Motion

℞ Retrograde
D Direct

1st Quarter/New Moon ☽
2nd Quarter ◑

3rd Quarter/Full Moon: ☺
4th Quarter ◐

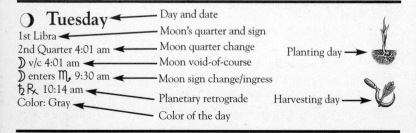

☽ **Tuesday** ← Day and date
1st Libra ← Moon's quarter and sign
2nd Quarter 4:01 am ← Moon quarter change
☽ v/c 4:01 am ← Moon void-of-course
☽ enters ♏ 9:30 am ← Moon sign change/ingress
♄ ℞ 10:14 am ← Planetary retrograde
Color: Gray ← Color of the day

Planting day →

Harvesting day →

The Witching Hour
by Gerina Dunwich

When the clock strikes twelve o'clock midnight, this is said to be the time when the restless spirits of the dead rise up out of their graves, strange and terrifying creatures of the supernatural walk the Earth, and the shadows of the occult grow their darkest and most powerful. But is there any truth behind such beliefs, or are they merely myths that have survived the passing of centuries?

The hour of midnight has long been known as the "witching hour," for this is when the clairvoyant and spellcasting powers of all Witches and sorcerers are believed to be at their peak. It is a special time of magic and transformation, as well as romance and mystery.

When Lady Luna is full and bright, midnight becomes a witching hour of the greatest power, and is the traditional time of the month for rituals such as "Drawing Down the Moon" to be held. The witching hour is also the traditional time for esbats to begin. An esbat is the monthly meeting of a Witches' coven, normally held thirteen times a year on either the Full or New Moon, depending on the coven's preference. During esbats, religious worship is conducted, business matters relating to the coven are discussed, and healings and magical spells are carried out. In most traditions of the Craft, a cakes-and-wine (or cakes-and-ale) ritual normally follows an esbat.

In ancient times, the power of the witching hour was applied not only to the casting of spells and bindings, but to divination, necromancy, spirit conjurations, shapeshifting, certain alchemical workings, the crafting of magical talismans and amulets, the constructing of ritual tools, and many other purposes.

Superstition and Folklore

The witching hour of midnight is not only a very magical time, but one surrounded by centuries of folklore, superstitious beliefs, and omens. It would be impossible to list them all, but some of the following examples are the most common superstitions.

It is considered a bad omen if a clock strikes thirteen times instead of twelve at the hour of midnight. Another version of this superstition holds that the thirteenth chime conjures up the Devil. And, in England, it is said that dire misfortune will find its way into the lives of the royal family within three months if London's Big Ben strikes irregularly at the midnight hour.

According to ancient legend, Witches can make themselves invisible or shapeshift into animals when the clock strikes twelve. Midnight is the transformational point when one day turns into the next, and in the minds of the ancients, this unequivocally linked the witching hour not only to the transformation of time, but to physical transformation—shapeshifting—as well.

It was believed that the witching hour could bring on a temporary fit of insanity known as "midnight madness" in certain individuals. This was often tied in with the Full Moon and its reputed power to produce lunacy (or "Moon madness").

In old European folklore, at the midnight hour—especially when the Moon was full—vampires woke from their dreamless slumber, ghouls roamed the graveyards, demons manifested, and cursed men transformed into werewolves to prowl the Earth in search of human victims. The living wouldn't be truly safe from the evil of these supernatural monstrosities until the first rays of dawn illuminated the horizon.

During the period in human history dominated by the bloodlust of the Inquisition, it was widely believed that sorcerers and sorceresses alike practiced the black arts when the witching hour was accompanied by a waning Moon. Curses, hexes, and other forms of maleficia

would be cast upon enemies to bring them bad luck and ruin. In some cases, it was believed, midnight sorcery during the waning Moon was used to deliver illness, insanity, accidents, and even death!

Contemporary Beliefs

The "veil between the worlds" is believed to be at its most thin at midnight, which explains why encounters with ghosts, faery folk, and other supernaturals occur most often during this time of the night. One of the most famous books on the practice of ceremonial magic is the medieval grimoire known as *The Key of Solomon*. According to this book of magical instructions, certain hours of the day and night rule and exert a powerful influence over certain planets. The planets corresponding to the midnight hour for each day of the week are as follows: the Sun on Sunday; the Moon on Monday; Mars on Tuesday; Mercury on Wednesday; Jupiter on Thursday; Venus on Friday; and Saturn on Saturday. It is believed that magical and mysterious events timed to correspond with these days have added power.

Traditionally, when the witching hour takes place on a night of the waxing Moon, this is the correct time for the casting of spells, the brewing of potions, and the working of charms to increase wealth, strengthen the physical body, attract good luck, inspire love and lust, and tune into psychic abilities. Most contemporary Witches and Pagans work with the power of the waning Moon to energize spells, potions, and charms that are designed for curing illnesses, banishing negativity and all manners of evil, binding those who do harm, lifting curses, breaking hexes, and reversing love spells.

A witching hour in the dark phase of the Moon is regarded by some occultists to be a dangerous time to work magic. It is associated with the ancient Pagan gods and goddesses of the underworld and the conjuration of all things evil. Many contemporary practitioners of the Craft avoid working magic at this time of the month.

Séances are traditionally held at midnight, for most spiritualists and mediums believe it is at this time, at the intersection of night and day, that the spirits of the dead grow restless and communication with the spirit world is best achieved. According to the published research of numerous paranormal investigators, the witching hour seems to be the prime time for most hauntings and poltergeist activity to occur.

Samhain / Halloween

The midnight hour of Halloween (the Witches' sabbat of Samhain) is a very special time. For centuries, this has been the traditional time for unmarried women and men to perform annual rituals of love divination to determine who their future spouses will be, and what they will be like. While most Halloween midnight divinations are concerned with matters of an amorous nature, there exist a number of divinatory methods in Ireland and parts of Great Britain used for determining whether a certain person will live to see the next Halloween.

Midnight on October 31 is also a time surrounded by a vast number of folk beliefs and superstitions. For instance, if you should hear footsteps following closely behind you at midnight on Halloween, take care not to turn around and look because it may be the Grim Reaper (or, in some versions, the Devil) coming to claim you. If a person casts no shadow at midnight on Halloween, this is said to be an omen of their death. Another old superstitious belief holds that the apparitions of all persons destined to die before the next Halloween can be observed walking through, or floating above, churchyards at the witching hour on All Hallows' Eve.

Witching Power

The witching hour is said to be the time when all spells, whether they be of black or white magic, take effect. The energies of the witching hour enhance all forms of magic, meditation, and divination, which is beneficial to all Witches and Pagans, regardless of their tradition.

There is no other time of the day or night that comes close to being as magical, mystical, and mysterious as the one known as the witching hour.

Planetary Stations
by Estelle Daniels

When you look in an astrological ephemeris (detailed tables of planetary placements) or an almanac, you occasionally see an ℞, S, or D listed next to a planet's symbol on certain days. Have you wondered what those are and how to use them? Those symbols indicate the direction (℞/retrograde or D/direct) and the degree, or position (S/station), of the planet when its direction changed. For example, ☿ ℞ 22 ♃ 48, tells you that Mercury is retrograde at 22 degrees and 48 minutes of Jupiter.

In our solar system, the planets, asteroids, and comets orbit around the Sun in an east to west direction at various speeds, depending on their size and distance from the Sun. The Moon, Earth's satellite, revolves around the Earth, but from the Earth it is not apparent that the planets revolve around the Sun. Instead, they appear to revolve around Earth. Sometimes we observe a planet appear to slow, then stop, and finally move backward against the stars. This is called retrograde movement (℞), but it is really an illusion. The planet did not actually stop, change direction, or go backward—it just seemed to from our point of view. An analogy is that of two cars on a highway. Both are moving forward, but one is moving faster than the other. The faster car appears to overtake the slower one. If you, in the faster car, view the slower car against the background, it appears to be moving backward relative to the horizon. After a time, the retrograde planet, like the car, will appear to slow again, then stop, and finally begin to move forward.

When this happens we say the planet has gone direct, and you'll see the symbol "D" along with the day and time next to the planet's position in an ephemeris.

When a planet is retrograde, its energy is different—slower, less overt—therefore, its action will be less obvious. For example, when Mercury is retrograde, your thinking processes may seem deeper and more sensitive. You might feel inclined to revisit places you've been before. It's also a good time to plan activities because you'll be more inclined to think things through and re-evaluate your decisions.

The degree at which a planet retrogrades, or goes direct, is more sensitized because the planet's apparent motion stopped and changed direction there. Just as an eclipse on or opposite a planet energizes and highlights the planet, the house in which it resides, and the matters and house(s) it rules, so will a planetary station increase that planet's energy. If Venus stations on your Moon, watch out for romance, some sort of sentimental dealings with a parent, a friend from the past, or maybe an ex-spouse to come into your life around the time of the station. The timing may be within a week on either side of the station, but something will be highlighted. See which houses are ruled by the Moon (Cancer) and Venus (Taurus and Libra) in your chart. Matters pertaining to those houses will also be highlighted. With the station degrees themselves, look only to Mercury, Venus, Mars, Jupiter, and Saturn for dramatic effects.

The outer planets, Jupiter, Saturn, Uranus, Neptune, and Pluto, retrograde four to five months each year. While their retrogrades don't have the immediate impact that Mercury, Venus, or Mars retrogrades do, they have an effect nonetheless. The three outermost planets, Uranus, Neptune, and Pluto, have a more subtle and less intense effect when they station. That's because they take much longer to orbit the Sun, and retrograde for up to five months, but just their passage over degrees is enough to cause change.

How can we take advantage of these planetary energies? First, check an ephemeris and note the days a planet stations. Things that happen on those days, or within a day or two, may tend to become prominent or important. Like eclipses, the stations intensify action, and unless you want chaos, change, and unexpected surprises—good or bad—it is best to keep to routine as much as possible. The planet is changing gears, and the things which that planet rules are about to change direction.

The most frequent and shortest retrograde is Mercury. Roughly three times a year, Mercury stations, goes retrograde for about three weeks, then stations and moves forward again until the next retrograde. Because Mercury rules communications and short distance travel, the mail, telephone systems, and cars can experience disruptions when its motion is retrograde. It's a good time to get to tasks you have been putting off until a rainy day—clean out closets, answer overdue correspondence, and so on. It isn't a good time to start new projects, sign a contract, or buy a car or computer.

Retrograde periods tend to rule anything which starts with "re-." For example, restarting, renewing, recalling, renovating, and recreating are actions you might take during a retrograde period. You might consider using retrograde energies if you want to reinforce a spell. Check your ephemeris to determine the motion of the planet that rules the matter, or you can use the Mercury retrograde for a general reinforcement. Issues related to the retrograding planet may not operate as smoothly during retrograde periods, but unexpected ideas, applications, and correspondences may spring up. What retrogrades do offer is opportunities to go over, review, and change what we have done. We can take a rest, look back, re-evaluate, see what worked and what didn't, and then think about plans for the future. Just wait for the direct motion to do new things.

Keep track of which planets are retrograde, and modify your activities accordingly. At the very least, be alert for those days when planets station. I have found that they are usually chaotic, rarely go pleasantly, and anything started or signed on those days is flawed or will require massive changes and revisions.

The stations of Venus and Mars were considered the most important in the ancient world. Their energies were seen as the strongest. Venus stations roughly every seventeen months for about six weeks. Mars stations less frequently, and for longer—roughly every twenty-five-and-a-half months for a little over two months. People born under a retrograde planet, especially Mercury, Venus, or Mars, usually see and experience the world more from the inside, out.

Many astrologers believe retrograde placements in a natal chart can indicate karmic issues and lessons brought from past lives. It is then reasoned that a chart with no retrograde planets shows a person starting life without karmic baggage. These people would, however, be focused on externals rather than on internal introspection. During those rare times when there are five or more planets retrograde, people should think about the past and where it can lead us, rather then just blithely moving forward.

Work with past lives, history, research, psychometry, and so on can be enhanced during a retrograde, especially of Mercury. If you want to get in touch with personal life lessons, do a working when a retrograde planet in your natal chart is currently retrograde in the sky. (It doesn't have to be in the same degree or sign as your natal chart.) This timing can give insight into those issues.

Retrograde is a part of the natural cycle of the planets as we experience them living on Earth. Start becoming aware of retrogrades, and see how their energies work with your magical activities. Blessed be.

Planetary Stations for 2001

January 25 ♄ D 24♉04	June 4 ☿ ℞ 29♊58
January 25 ♃ D 1♊11	June 28 ☿ D 21♊16
February 4 ☿ ℞ 0♓34	July 19 ♂ D 15♐06
February 25 ☿ D 15♒25	August 23 ♇ D 12♐32
March 9 ♀ ℞ 17♈44	September 27 ♄ ℞ 14♊58
March 18 ♇ ℞ 15♐16	October 1 ☿ ℞ 29♎41
April 20 ♀ D 1♈27	October 18 ♆ D 5♒59
May 11 ♆ ℞ 8♒47	October 23 ☿ D 14♎12
May 11 ♂ ℞ 29♐03	October 30 ♅ D 20♒54
May 29 ♅ ℞ 24♒50	November 2 ♃ ℞ 15♑41

Modernizing Ancient Holidays

by Breid Foxsong

By firelight and candle's glow, by broom and bell and knife, the ancient ways are brought into in modern lives. Why do we cling to seventeenth-century garb and tools in this modern age? Is the use of ancient tools and symbols a touchstone to the past? Or is there more to it than that?

We no longer need to cast spells to hold the cart axles together or create charms to keep the oxen from colic. Instead we chant to keep the car running and make talismans to protect our computers from a virus. Air conditioning and radiant heat make it more comfortable inside, and easy to ignore the turning of the wheel of the year. Certainly light bulbs are more convenient and safer to use than open flames, and water is available now at the turning of a tap rather than by breaking ice or hauling buckets. But we still live in a world with changing seasons and, especially in the modern day, we must be careful not to lose touch with the world around us. How can we use the advantages of modern times and still stay in tune with the ancient cycles?

The obvious way that the modern world has touched paganism is through the Internet. You can jump on the information highway and find rituals for all occasions (and a few for just plain silliness!). You can find spells for things that never occurred to you: banishing your dust bunnies, for example, or blessing your fish tank. Transactions and friendships with people across the country, or even across the world, are possible. Many Pagans are doing ritual in large groups, or even forming covens, without ever meeting face to face. But does this help us? Or make it easier to separate our mundane lives from our spiritual ones? To practice a religion of nature, you must be in touch with the world around you. If what you do in circle doesn't become a part of your everyday life, is it truly a religion? To bring the ancient cycles into the modern world is to build a bridge of ourselves, a personal connection between your self and the land. Not the land of your ancestors, but the land that you, yourself, are dwelling in. This may not be fields and forests, but rather the streets and suburbs we live and work in. And it's not just an "eight holidays a year" process, but a day-to-day celebration of life and Deity.

Each sabbat was originally about the changing of the seasons in a particular locale. The rain and sunshine cycles of Florida are very different from the snow and thaw cycles of northern Michigan, and should be celebrated differently. However, the sabbats are about the changes in the human life cycle as well. We may not have our personal cycles and changes as tidily as dates on a calendar, but still, each of us goes through the rites of passage reflected in the wheel of the year. Humans are always a part of Mother Nature. Our lives mirror hers, and hers mirrors ours.

Since we must deal with a calendar year when we deal with the real world, lets start with Yule. The longest night is upon us, heating bills are high, and the tendency is to cuddle close to your heater. Although this is called "midwinter," for most of the country, the coldest times are yet to come. The Yule tree is a symbol of the coming spring and deserves to be given reverence. Make a journey out to a tree farm and cut your own tree, promising it the splendor of lights and decorations, and a final resting place as a part of your garden or, at the very least, as mulch. Decorate with wheels, Sun symbols, and splashes of color against the green, black, and white of a winter landscape. Make an outdoor circle with a ring of greenery or straw that can be burned during ritual to warm the body and soul and encourage the Sun to return. If you live in an area that doesn't snow, take advantage of the warm, solar symbols of an orange tree, with its brightness and sunny orange cheer, and decorate that instead!

Yule is a time to look inward: start doing daily meditations or take up a contemplative activity such as tai chi. For our ancestors, this was a time of retreat. We can't do that now, but we can plan to use such isolation as is available for growing inwardly. This is the rebirth of the Sun: let it be the rebirth of something that you always wanted to do, but haven't pursued. Were you the best jacks player in the third grade? Buy a set and see if your skills have remained. Or sit by a fire and watch the snow or rain fall, and focus on the world around you. If you tend to complain about the weather, think of one thing you like about the season. Then think of another. Allow the spirituality of the resting time to permeate your life. Use your imagination!

Imbolc, Candlemas, is the time of light without heat. I think of this as the cold clear light of a winter day. It's really an agricultural holiday, based on the lactation time of sheep, but in modern times it's marked by the appearance of seed catalogs in the mailbox. In my part of the country, this is the deepest part of winter. It is the time when we are buried in snow, cold, and ice. So I celebrate Imbolc by going to the local botanical gardens and forgetting winter for an hour or so. This is a birth time, a time to focus on the creative spirit.

The goddess generally honored at this time is Brigit, a triple goddess of poetry, healing, and smith craft. Honoring her in modern times can be easily done by reading a book (especially one regarding a new interest or field). Acquiring healing skills doesn't have to be mystical to be sacred—you can take a first aid class, or a class in CPR. The ancient art of smithing is honored on a daily basis in the miracle of automobiles. Do you know how the magic of the combustion engine works?

At the Spring Equinox, most of the U.S. is experiencing the storm season. Light and dark are battling in the flash of lightning across the

clouds. But the season is definitely mellowing, and the earth is starting to open herself to seed. Bulbs are blooming, and some trees are budding out. Maple syrup is a good way to celebrate the rising of the sap. The smell of wet earth is all around us. This is a good time to get out and dig your toes into the cold mud that is everywhere. Yes, it's usually too cold to go barefoot, but touch the earth! Dig your fingers into it!

Coloring eggs is a spring activity, even if you don't have children to give you an excuse. Make an egg tree with the dyed eggs, or paint runes on them and use them as divination tools. Rabbit planters or bunny candlesticks can often be found on sale after the Christian holiday of Easter. Since the rabbit or hare is a terrific symbol of fertility and spring, you may want to use these on your altar or as guardians around the circle. Geese are a good fertility symbol as well, and also indicate the return of spring by flocking toward the North.

Take a walk on your lunch break and notice the flora around you. Even the most urban dweller has a tree somewhere nearby, and often will see an ambitious weed or two working its way though the cracks in the sidewalk. Look out the window. Do the trees look different? Softer? Does the pattern of light change in your office? This is a time to open your senses to the awakening world. The spring is marked by the migration patterns; geese flying north, college kids flying south. Let them bring the renewal back to you, even if you can't go with them.

Beltane is the most popular of the Pagan holidays, and the one that has kept the most earthy meaning. This is a time to create. This is the holiday where random acts of kindness to total strangers is most appropriate. Is sex a part of Beltane? Yes, but remember that "all acts of love and pleasure" are the rituals of the Goddess. Love and pleasure can be a good meal, a game of laser-tag, flying a kite, or shutting yourself into the bathroom for a three-hour soak. Make a Maypole and invite friends to come and dance. Hold a backyard barbecue. Bring flowers to your secretary (or your boss), "just because." Send a present or a card to someone you haven't spoken with in a while. The practice of exchanging May baskets is out of fashion, but is still a lot of fun.

Even if your seasons don't change much, look for the subtle signs of the coming summer. The temperatures are rising, and the sunshine is slowly changing color toward the warmth of summer. What events are happening in the world around you? Remember that, no matter what your season, this ought to be a religion of Nature. Guide your inner self by what Nature is doing.

Litha, or Midsummer, is really the beginning of the summer for most of North America. Like Yule, it's a holiday that is more focused on

what is to come than on what is actually happening now. Litha is about learning to balance our lives between flesh and spirit, and the need to keep one foot on the ground if you want your head in the clouds. Whether or not we like them, there need to be limits for anything to be successful. Unbalanced growth kills an ecosystem. By defining boundaries, we can shape our lives to give us both structure and personal identity. We cannot, alas, play forever, but work also requires time off in order to be most productive.

Community service is a good way of giving back what we have received. Do you volunteer regularly? Think about how your talents could help the area around you. Offer to weed the flowerbed at your children's local school during the summer months, or take the neighborhood kids to the zoo. This is a holiday of potentials, a focus on things that are on their way. Go back and look at your personal goals for the year. Are you accomplishing them? Store the winter clothing, and the winter attitudes, and clean the house of any shadows. This is a good time of year to scrub the walls and wash the ceilings. If you are painting rooms, consider the implications of your paint colors. Are you painting magic onto the walls?

Sunflowers and daisies are great symbols of the season. Sunflower seeds can be mixed into the Circle cakes, and petals or flower designs can be drawn on top. You can also weave dandelion or daisy chains to be the perimeter of a circle, to go around the top of the altar, or to just drape around things. This is a good meditation device: as you weave the chains, you weave the magic. Both the Green Mother and the Green Man are in power, so you might make a green gown or drape for any statuettes on your altar.

Lammas begins the harvest. Make a ceremonial trip to the grocery store, and "gather" the food that will take you into the winter. You can't do it all in one trip, obviously, but make some choices based on the coming months. Consider the people that were a part of getting this food to you. Thank them, at least in spirit, as you choose the cans and bags that are part of the modern harvest. If you really want to honor your ancestors, go to the county fair! The medieval jugglers and minstrels are today's midway "carnies" and sideshow entertainers. The animal exhibits let you recognize the importance of the farmer in today's world, and you can appreciate the time and energy that goes into the canning, baking, preserving, and displaying of the foods that win the prizes. Don't be surprised if it's an apartment neighbor winning one of those ribbons—you don't have to have a farm kitchen to bake a wonderful pie!

Lammas is a festival celebrating grain. It is also a feast day, so a community or family dinner is in order either before, after, or during any ritual. Another aspect of grain is seen in the recent popularity of cornfield mazes—advertised for families, but an incredible ritual experience if approached in the right fashion. Check your local paper for one near you. Early in the morning or late in the evening is usually the best time to go so that you won't be overwhelmed by giggling kids. Or just incorporate the giggling kids right into your walking meditation. They are, after all, no worse than the dragons that our ancestors wrote into the maps.

Mabon is a settling time. Children go back to school, leaves begin to drop to the ground, and the abundance of the harvest is beginning to dwindle. Hurricane season is coming and the start of the fall migrations is overhead. This is a time of preparation. Do you have an emergency kit packed? Enough supplies that, if you were kept in the house by early winter weather, you would be warm and cozy?

The gardens are beginning to go to compost and the light is changing once again to a honey-golden tone. Traditionally this is a time of sacrifice: we give back to the land as a thanks for having received. We aren't sacrificing our cattle and crops now, but you can sacrifice that old out-of-style jacket and the sweaters you no longer wear to a shelter for the homeless. Sacrifice some time to do the chores you hate the most. Offer up an evening with your sweetie and do the things he or she most enjoys. Fertilize the lawn and plants, and begin to plan for mulching and digging in.

If you're wondering what to do with all those extra zucchini from the garden, why not use them as wand or athame substitutes? Carve your names in runes and use them to add a lighthearted touch, and you can use corn or wheat stalks to draw the circle, in place of a staff or sword. Since Mabon is often seen as a ritual of the West, you can use images of water as a focus. The maturity and depth of the ocean or the laughter and energy of a fastmoving stream provide different, but equally powerful, emotions. For those that don't have access to a lake or an ocean, there is always the hot tub—a very modern ritual!

The Equinox is a time of harmony as well as balance. Songs, chants, and dances are particularly appropriate now. A song written in celebration and love and sung with joy is beautiful, no matter how tone-deaf the singer. Harmony should be savored in all things. Take a moment before eating to enjoy the sight and smell of good food. Notice. Appreciate. Learn. Grow. Give thanks.

By Samhain, the fall colors are gone. Nature is down to the essentials. This is the time of cold and darkness. This is the time for clearing out the deadfall and dross in our lives and going back to basics. Take a personal inventory. Are you where you want to be in your life? Take a look around you. How much of your surroundings are just clutter? Do you need to clean house and get rid of energies and leftover emotions? Even in those areas that do not experience extremes of temperature, there are changes in the sunlight and the attitudes. For southern areas, this is the time when you can finally turn the air conditioner off or take the fans down. In some parts of California, the butterflies are returning for the winter. Mourning is done, not only for the people who have crossed into the Summerland, but also for those things that have gone by the wayside—friendships lost (or found), changes in lifestyle or in jobs, or any major transformation that has entered your life.

In the modern world, the focus at this time is on children and candy, but carving pumpkins and putting up cornstalks are not only to entertain the trick-or-treaters, but also to bring light and harvest to our homes. Choose your "treats" well, because the gifts of food represent the abundance you hope to receive: this is symbolism at its best!

To celebrate the transcendence of life, brightly colored leaves can be woven into wreaths and draped across windows, mantles, or even doorways. You can display flowers and fall leaves together to make a subtle Pagan statement that even the most strict of non-Pagans would approve. Acorns, walnuts, and other seeds can add to the symbolism. Death is life is death, even in the new millennium.

Modern or ancient, face to face or by computer, the Craft is always growing and changing. By keeping in mind the principles behind the sabbats and the cycles of life, both without and within, we can grow and change along with them. The ancient religion is thriving and strong in a modern world and, to quote a popular Pagan chant, "Everything lost is found again, in a new form, in a new way." May our new ways be as productive and long lasting as our old ones!

May Day
by Jami Shoemaker

When I was a little girl, my sister and I would celebrate the first of May by making little paper baskets and filling them with candy. We would then sneak around the neighborhood to our friends' houses, leave them on the doorsteps, ring the bells, and run away, screaming with laughter. The trick was never to reveal your identity to the recipient of the gift. Little did I know at the time that we were celebrating an old custom that hearkened back to ancient times.

Origins

Like any celebration based on ancient agricultural practices, it is impossible to know the exact origins of our modern May Day. Celebrations of spring are found in cultures all over the world, with similar themes of renewal, planting and growth, the gathering of flowers, and playful celebration.

However, much of the meaning behind modern Pagan customs can be traced to Celtic origins, or at least what we attribute to the Celts. We know that they divided the year into two seasons: summer and winter, the dark and the light halves of the year. Within this, they honored four major turning points, Samhain, Imbolc, Beltane, and Lughnasadh, with fire festivals.

These festivals coincided astrologically with the Sun at 15 degrees Scorpio, Aquarius, Taurus, and Leo, respectively. This made these pivotal points each a type of "movable feast" originally, like the solstices and equinoxes, which vary by a day or two from year to year. But due to changes in calendars over time, eventually the first day of the months of November, February, May, and August were earmarked for these festivals, evolving into what Witches call the Great Sabbats, with the celebrations commencing at sunset on the eve before.

The flexibility in the actual date is still followed by some Pagans today, and May Day, or Beltane, celebrations calculated in this way are called "Old Beltane." This explains the custom in ancient Ireland of celebrating the first day of summer on May 6. This day was given to Inghean Bhuidhe, the Yellow-Haired Girl, one of three sister-goddesses who brought in the seasons: the First of Spring, the First of Summer, and the First Harvest.

The return of the light was called Cetsamhain ("opposite Samhain") or Bealtaine in Ireland, Galan-Mai in Wales, and in Scotland, Beaultiunn. On the Isle of Man, it was known as Day of Summer, and in Germany, Walpurgisnacht. The medieval church renamed the holiday Roodmas, hoping to shift the emphasis from the phallic Maypole to the Holy Rood, or Cross, and celebrations once marked by Pagan frivolity were usurped by festivities held in churchyards.

Ancient Customs

Beltane (Anglicized spelling) is a fire festival, and was dedicated to the god of light, called variously Bel, Balor, Belenos, and Baldur. It marked the beginning of the summer season, and the return of the Sun to light and nourish the earth. Among the customs associated with the Celtic celebration of Beltane (literally, "Bel's fire") is the lighting of two fires on a hilltop. The Druids gathered wood from nine different trees to make their fire every year on top of Tara Hill in County Meath, Ireland. Traditionally, all other fires were extinguished, and relit from

these sacred "need fires" as an act of renewal. Before cattle were taken into the open pasture for summer they were driven either between the fires or through the ashes to purify them of disease, and men and women would leap the flames for protection, and for luck in matters of fertility, romance, and home.

This brings us to perhaps the most significant part of the Beltane customs—that of fertility and growth. With the return of light and warmth, the earth's fertility was assured for another season. This mystery was seen as the union of earth and sky, or Goddess and God. The fruit of this union was seen in the greening of the countryside, and in the harvest to come. This coming together of the forces of nature was honored as the "Sacred Marriage" of the Goddess and God. Imitating their union was the ultimate act of worship, and ensured the continuance of the community.

In light of this "marriage of the gods," Pagan weddings, or "handfastings" were popular at this time of year. This was the commitment of a year and a day, giving couples a sort of "trial run" at marriage, and after that time both parties could agree to a long-term relationship, or could go their separate ways without remorse.

For those looking only, perhaps, for an evening's frolicking, the "greenwood marriage" was popular. Young men and women would spend the night at the Beltane fires, or would go into the woods on Beltane Eve, gathering garlands and flowers, making love, and staying up to greet the Sun. If a woman were lucky, she would find herself with child, as children conceived on May Eve were considered favored by the gods. These "greenwood marriages" continued long after the Christian form of marriage replaced the peasants' handfasting. May Eve was a time to drop all inhibitions and enjoy unbridled sexuality. No rules applied. Even married or handfasted couples would relax their commitment for this one night.

Symbols of fertility abounded at May time—the greening of the woods, the flowering of the plants, the mating of the animals. Perhaps one of the most blatant symbols of fertility is the Maypole, traditionally cut and carried from the forest by the village's most virile young men. Though the symbol of the Maypole is universal (the living tree representing the growth that awakens with spring), the tradition of erecting a Maypole may stem from an ancient Roman tree-giving custom. It has been said that the erection of the Maypole, which includes burying one end in the earth, is yet another representation of the union of the gods.

Beltane falls exactly opposite Hallows, which marks the beginning of the dark half of the year. These two turning points were seen as extremely powerful times in the wheel of the year. They fell on the "in-between" times, embodying the mysteries of light and dark, life and death, and the transitions between. It is at these times when the veil between the worlds of spirit and matter, the dead and the living, are the thinnest. Beltane was then associated with great magic. This was a time for divination, and for spells that would bring love and prosperity. It was also a time when the faery folk were more easily seen. Their appearance could bring good fortune, or, if a mortal were enticed by their mischievous ways, he or she might fall into a trance and be taken to a place beyond time.

Roman Influence

The month of May takes its name from the goddess Maia, who appears in both Greek and Roman mythologies. In Greece, she was "grandmother," "midwife," or "wise one" and she was known as the mother of Hermes. The Romans associated her with their fire goddess of the same name who, along with Flora and Feronia, ruled growth and warmth, including sexual desire. Maia's day was the first of May, and the associations with growth can still be seen in the Christian dedication of the month to Mary, Queen of Flowers.

When the Romans came to Britain, they brought with them their own ancient spring rites. The goddess Flora was worshiped as the embodiment of the flowering of all of nature, including human. She was the queen of plants, the goddess of flowers, and the patron of Roman prostitutes. Flora was honored during a week-long festival from April 28–May 3. The Floralia included the gathering of flowers, used in processions, dances, and games. Young men raced to see who could be the first to hang a wreath on Flora's statue, and wrap garlands around the columns of her temple. The female body was especially honored at this time. Graphic, erotic medallions were distributed, and public orgies celebrated the fruitfulness of the earth. The "festival of nude women" was celebrated until the third century CE, when Roman authorities demanded the celebrants be clothed. The sense of unrestrained freedom was even enjoyed by Roman slaves on this day, with the stipulation that they return to their masters' houses that night.

Medieval & Tudor Britain

May Day found great popularity in medieval and Tudor times. Women rose before sunrise and went into the field to bathe their faces in the dew—an act believed to enhance beauty and restore a youthful complexion. Hawthorne was associated with May, and the gathering of Hawthorn boughs was known as "going a-Maying." Accompanied by song, dance, and general merriment, the hawthorn boughs were brought back to the village, and used to garland the throne of the May Queen, a young woman of the village crowned "Queen" for the day.

This custom seems to hearken back to the celebrations of Flora, keeping alive the knowledge of the goddess of growth and flowers. Flowers gathered on May Eve would be left at houses in the village, in exchange for food and drink. Our custom of leaving baskets on doorsteps has its roots in this tradition. The flower-bearers were seen as messengers of spring, and it was thought that those who rewarded  them with generosity were assured abundance in the coming season.

Along with the Queen of May, spectators were also entertained by Robin Hood, Maid Marian, Friar Tuck, and other characters modeled from old Pagan customs of the gods of the greenwood. Other festivities included games, sports, archery contests, and morris dancing. Carols heralding the arrival of spring were sung, and children paraded about carrying a doll dressed in white—the "Lady of May."

People of the villages decorated their homes with wreaths and garlands, and a Maypole, cut by the young men and carried into town with great ceremony, was set up in the village square. Some of these poles reached enormous heights, as villages competed to have the tallest pole. Ribbons and other decorations were added, and the practice of dancing around the Maypole and weaving the ribbons together has become one of our most beloved traditions.

Modern Celebrations

Many ancient customs can be seen in current celebrations of May Day. Pagan practices embrace the Maypole, dancing, and bonfires of the past, and honor the union of Goddess and God. The magic of the warming earth, the bright greens of the woods, and the giddiness of life returning are as universally inspiring as ever. Whether it's celebrated as Labor Day in Russia, Vappu in Finland, Flores de Mayo in El Salvador, or Flittin' Day in Scotland, May Day is still a time for relaxing the rules and celebrating spring, even if that simply means going barefoot for the first time that year. And, yes, some children still leave May baskets on the doorsteps of friends' houses and run away, squealing with delight.

Monthly Correspondences

by Yasmine Galenorn

When we look at the modern year, we see each month as a separate unit with its own energy and correspondences. This guide correlates each month to a particular theme, complete with guidelines for flowers, stones, affirmations, deities, and more. Use it to create monthly rituals, or to make some of the colder months a bit more fun.

January

Winter in the northern hemisphere tends to have colder days and longer nights. We've passed the revelry of the holidays and now are faced with a long haul till spring. During this period, it's good to focus on new beginnings, and on cleansing our lives, our space, and our insight as we look toward the New Year with excitement and a renewed sense of setting goals.

Stone: Garnet
Flower: Carnation
Incense: Sage
Color: White
Moon: Wolf

Holiday: New Year's Day
Fruit: Coconut
Goddesses: Jana, Nuit, Lakshmi
Gods: Janus, Ukko, Zeus

I manifest new chances for good fortune, clarity, and insight. I open myself to new experience and allow change to manifest in my life.

February

The focus turns to healing as we prepare our bodies for the busy seasons to come. We sense renewal in the air, we see the snowdrops and crocuses peek through the snow. Now we turn toward ourselves and say, "What do I need in order to be healthy this year? What should I change in my diet, my exercise routine, my life, to ensure abundant energy and strength this summer?"

Stone: Amethyst   **Holiday**: Imbolc
Flower: Violet   **Fruit**: Apple
Incense: Lavender   **Goddesses**: Brighid, Isis, Kuan Yin
Color: Blue   **Gods**: Thoth, Apollo
Moon: Ice

I strengthen myself, I heal myself, I listen to my body.

March

Now is the time we see new growth all around us: a rebirth of leaf and branch, and young animals creeping out of the woods and barns to meet the world. We can plan gardens and the summer's projects, and use this month as a springboard to launch the new ideas that we formulated in January. With the renewed health we began working on in February, we'll have the strength to follow through.

Stone: Aquamarine   **Holiday**: Ostara
Flower: Daffodil   **Fruit**: Fig
Incense: Poppy   **Goddesses**: Eostre, Flora
Color: Green   **Gods**: Green Man, Osiris, Frey
Moon: Storm

My life is filled with growth and virility.

April

During April, we take some time to sit back and enjoy what we've done so far this year. We rest for a bit, letting what we've put in motion chug along. The effort has been made; now we can wait and watch the results grow. Then, as we see the success of our past projects, we can plan our future endeavors. We can look at April as a month during which we intermingle play with work, never letting go of our goals yet always taking a few moments to bask in the springtime breezes and the scent of freshly turned sod.

Stone: Diamond
Flower: Sweet Pea
Incense: Hyacinth
Color: Dark Blue
Moon: Growing

Holiday: Walpurgis Night
Fruit: Quince
Goddesses: Bast, White Tara, Idun
Gods: Ganesha, Tien Kuan, Vishnu

My life is working out more exquisitely than I could plan.

May

We feel our blood quicken, and we catch our breath at the sight of our mates or loved ones during the time of Beltane. Our bodies sense the rhythms of the season, and long to touch and be touched. We lose track of our thoughts at times. We must work, but our instincts urge us to run wild through the forest. Let yourself revel in the season, experience the pleasures of the body, and connect with the passion of our world.

Stone: Emerald
Flower: Lily
Incense: Patchouli
Color: Burgundy
Moon: Hare

Holiday: Beltane
Fruit: Avocado
Goddesses: Aphrodite, Pombagira
Gods: Pan, Priapus, Krishna

I am passionate and magnetic. I radiate strength, beauty, and poise.

June

Midsummer's Eve is upon us; the Sidhe and other faery folk run wild. Even as during May we felt our sexuality and sensuality heighten, now we see these feelings transformed into love, caring, and the sparkling magic of faery. The Fey are a feral race. They may lead you astray, play tricks, or turn you round and round, but they'll never bore you. Respect them. And leave a bowl of milk out for them on Midsummer's Eve. June also promises the time of fidelity and heart-matches. Weddings and handfastings abound under the honey-Moon, and the warmth of the Sun sparks thoughts of love.

Stone: Moonstone
Flower: Rose
Incense: Rose
Color: Red
Moon: Mead

Holiday: Litha
Fruit: Peach
Goddesses: Titania, Rhiannon
Gods: Dagda, Oak King, Oberon

I attract love and faery magic to my life.

July

We have passed the zenith of growth, and it is time to bask in the heat of the Sun as crops ripen, children play, and we migrate to beach and shore in search of the ocean mother. We also take another journey at this time, one focused within ourselves. July gives us a good time to seek our own truth, to go in search of our inner guidance.

Stone: Ruby
Flower: Delphinium
Incense: High John
Color: Indigo
Moon: Hay

Holiday: Lobster
Fruit: Grapes
Goddesses: Nephthys, Viviane
Gods: Dionysus, Myrddin, Taliesin

As above, so below. I seek my answers within the labyrinth of myself.

August

Though the heat remains, there is a faint golden tinge to the sunlight and we can sense that the season is waning and the light withdrawing. August is a time to look at our lives, see what is outworn and outdated, and cast those things aside, for we need no extra baggage to weigh us down as we journey into the darker half of the year.

Stone: Peridot
Flower: Gladiolus
Incense: Copal
Color: Gold
Moon: Corn

Holiday: Lughnasadh
Fruit: Blackberries
Goddesses: Cerridwen, Ishtar
Gods: Lugh, Dumuzi, Tammuz

I willingly sacrifice that which is outworn and outdated in my life.

September

We gather our abundance, the fruit of our labor, to stockpile for the winter and share with friends and family. We join hands in thanking the gods for seeing us through the season of plenty. We tie up loose ends from our gardens, and prepare for the season of intellect and cerebral work standing before us.

Stone: Sapphire　　　　**Holiday**: Mabon
Flower: Aster　　　　　**Fruit**: Banana
Incense: Cinnamon　　　**Goddesses**: Demeter, Ceres, Gaia
Color: Brown　　　　　 **Gods**: Adonis, Jupiter, Thor
Moon: Harvest

I reap the harvest for the work I've done. I enjoy the fruits of my labors.

October

We near the Pagan new year as we finish another turn of the wheel. It's time to prepare for the festival of the dead. During this time, we hear the call of the wild hunt, the distant sound of the dark gods on the wind. They stir our blood, send shivers up our spines, and remind us of our mortality.

Stone: Opal　　　　　 **Holiday**: Great Horn Fair (Herne)
Flower: Calendula　　　**Fruit**: Orange
Incense: Primrose　　　 **Goddesses**: Mielikki, Artemis
Color: Purple　　　　　**Gods**: Herne, Cernunnos, Odin
Moon: Blood

I hunt for the hidden answers. I seek my shadow to find all sides of myself.

November

Samhain heralds November with a solemn knell, as we revere and honor our ancestors. We take a moment to catch our breaths, and then begin preparations for Yule, and focus on our work and our families. During November, we enjoy curling up in a big chair with a good book and our best four-footed friend.

Stone: Topaz	**Holiday**: Samhain
Flower: Chrysanthemum	**Fruit**: Pomegranate
Incense: Gum Mastic	**Goddesses**: Hel, Tuonetar
Color: Black	**Gods**: Hades, Pluto, Tuoni
Moon: Snow	

Death into life; life into death. I understand the nature of existence.

December

Ice on the windows, cinnamon in the kitchen. December brings a focus on hearth and home. We celebrate the joys of family and friends, we decorate with ornaments to keep the austerity of winter at bay. We remember those less fortunate than ourselves, and welcome the rebirth of the Sun King, knowing that light will come again.

Stone: Turquoise	**Holiday**: Yule
Flower: Narcissus	**Fruit**: Cranberry
Incense: Bayberry	**Goddesses**: Hestia, Shasti, Rauni
Color: Silver	**Gods**: Holly King, Tapio, Horus
Moon: Cold	

I connect with and enjoy the company of my loved ones and friends.

January

1 Monday

1st ♓
☽ v/c 6:36 am
☽ enters ♈ 5:14 pm
Color: Silver

New Year's Day
Kwanzaa ends
Birthday of Sir James Frazer,
author of *The Golden Bough*

○ Tuesday

1st ♈
2nd Quarter 5:31 pm
Color: Red

For salt-reduced diets, use
lovage as a salt-substitute flavoring

3 Wednesday

2nd ♈
☽ v/c 5:09 am
♀ enters ♓ 1:14 pm
Color: Yellow

Death of Edgar Cayce, psychic

4 Thursday

2nd ♈
☽ enters ♉ 1:57 am
Color: Turquoise

Aquarian Tabernacle Church
registered in Australia by
Lady Tamara Von Forslun, 1994

5 Friday

2nd ♉
☽ v/c 9:09 pm
Color: Pink

6 Saturday

2nd ♉
☽ enters ♊ 6:44 am
Color: Blue

Twelfth Night/Epiphany
Patricia Crowther's Witchcraft
radio show, *A Spell of Witchcraft*,
airs in Britain, 1971

7 Sunday

2nd ♊
☽ v/c 2:19 pm
Color: Orange

If, as I read among very many writers, what
the Persians call magician is what we call
priest, what crime is it, I ask you, to be a
magician and to have thorough knowledge
and understanding and skill in the laws of
ceremonials, the proper form of sacred rites,
the ordinances of religious practices?
—Apuleius

January

8 Monday

2nd ♊
☽ enters ♋ 8:09 am
Color: White

Death of Dion Fortune, 1946

Birthday of MacGregor Mathers,
one of the three original founders
of the Golden Dawn, 1854

☺ Tuesday

2nd ♋
Full Moon 3:24 pm
Color: Gray

Cold Moon

Lunar Eclipse 3:22 pm, 19° ♋ 39'

Jamie Dodge wins lawsuit against
the Salvation Army, which fired her
based on her Wiccan religion, 1989

---

10 Wednesday

3rd ♋
☽ v/c 7:39 am
☽ enters ♌ 7:44 am
☿ enters ♒ 8:26 am
Color: Peach

---

11 Thursday

3rd ♌
☽ v/c 10:08 pm
Color: White

To keep the evil eye from casting its glare
upon you, carry a mojo bag filled with sage

---

12 Friday

3rd ♌
☽ enters ♍ 7:26 am
Color: Rose

Mary Smith hanged in England; she
had quarreled with neighbors, who
said that the Devil appeared
to her as a black man, 1616

Cold Moon

The silent, hoarfrost cold of winter creates an atmosphere in which you can work to reach your highest potential. January's Cold Moon is the perfect time to put the freeze on all your less-than-desirable habits: anger, resentment, criticism, guilt, substance-abuse, and other addictive behaviors. Make a New Year's resolution this year to eliminate actions that cause more harm than good, and use this simple ritual to freeze your problems:

Gather your ritual tools: a white candle, Zip-Lock freezer bag, pen, pitcher of water, and a sheet of white paper. Find a time and quiet place where you can perform your work.

Light the candle and pray over the water. Ask your gods, goddesses, and guiding spirits for assistance with your purpose. Write down all your negative behaviors, nine times each, on the paper. Fold the paper into a small square, and place it into the Zip-Lock bag. Fill the bag with enough prayer water to saturate and cover the paper. Put the bag in your freezer, say goodbye to your bad habits, and thank all for helping you.

—Marguerite Elsbeth

---

13 Saturday
3rd ♍
☽ v/c 11:12 pm
Color: Gray

Final witchcraft laws
repealed in Austria, 1787

---

14 Sunday
3rd ♍
☽ enters ♎ 9:05 am
Color: Yellow

Official Confession of Error by
jurors of Salem Witch Trials, 1696

Human Be-In, a Pagan-style festival,
takes place in San Francisco, attended by
Timothy Leary and Allen Ginsberg, 1967

January

15 Monday
3rd ♎
Color: Lavender

Birthday of Martin Luther King, Jr.
(observed)

☽ Tuesday
3rd ♎
4th Quarter 7:35 am
☽ v/c 7:35 am
☽ enters ♏ 2:02 pm
Color: White

Birthday of Dr. Dennis Carpenter,
Circle Sanctuary

17 Wednesday
4th ♏
Color: Brown

She is capable of bringing down the
sky, suspending the earth, making
the springs dry up, sweeping away
mountains, conjuring the spirits of the
dead; She can weaken the gods, put
out the stars, light up Hell itself.
—Apuleius describing a Witch
in *Metamorphoses*

18 Thursday
4th ♏
☽ v/c 8:44 pm
☽ enters ♐ 10:35 pm
Color: Violet

*Polish your magical wand with sandalwood
oil to enliven and escalate its powers*

19 Friday
4th ♐
☉ enters ♒ 7:16 pm
Color: Peach

Sun enters Aquarius
Birthday of Dorothy Clutterbuck,
who initiated Gerald Gardner

Set in Eastern Standard Time (EST)

January

I am that sweet place of regeneration
Of peaceful dreaming and pure relaxation
Of resting from tasks both hard and long
A place to recoup and fix what is wrong
Where Spirit controls every energy tide
And magic is born and flows in the ride
Where visions and dreams begin to unfold
And brand new reality forms to take hold
Where Creative forces regain their power
And potency grows by minute and hour
Nothing's impossible without or within
If you'll only relax and let it flow in
                               —Dorothy Morrison

---

20 Saturday
4th ♐
☽ v/c 1:18 pm
Color: Brown

Inauguration Day

---

21 Sunday
4th ♐
☽ enters ♑ 9:57 am
Color: Peach

Celtic Tree Month of Rowan begins

January

22 Monday

4th ♑

Color: Gray

To feel courageous, wear a corsage
composed of fresh borage blossoms

23 Tuesday

4th ♑

☽ v/c 10:38 am

☽ enters ♒ 10:43 pm

Color: Red

Birthday of Marija Gimbutas,
anthropologist

☽ Wednesday

4th ♒

New Moon 8:07 am

♄ D 7:24 pm

Color: White

Chinese New Year (snake)

25 Thursday

1st ♒

♃ D 3:38 am

Color: Green

O malady, disappear into the heavens:
pain, rise up to the clouds: inflamed
vapor, fly into the air, in order that the
wind may take thee away, that the tempest
may chase thee to distant regions, where
neither sun nor moon give their light.
—Incantation against sickness
from the *Kalevala*

26 Friday

1st ♒

☽ v/c 12:28 am

☽ enters ♓ 11:39 am

Color: Rose

Stress Tea

1 tsp. English Breakfast tea
1 tsp. chamomile, dried
1 tsp. elder flower, dried and crushed
2 tsp. hops, dried and crushed
2 tsp. rose hips, dried
1 tsp. valerian root, dried and crushed

Here is a good tea for days when stress seems overwhelming. You can make the tea in an automatic tea maker or use two pots, straining the herbs from one into the other with boiling water. Before you pour the tea, swirl it in the pot and say:

> Chase away pain and stress
> Chase away all duress
> Chase away the negative
> Open up the positive.

—Ann Moura

---

27 Saturday
1st ♓
Color: Indigo

---

28 Sunday
1st ♓
☽ v/c 2:48 pm
☽ enters ♈ 11:35 pm
Color: Gold

Scatter black cohosh leaves in the corner
of a room to evict a negative energy force

January/February

29 Monday
1st ♈
Color: Silver

There was a current belief that
Witches could sail in an eggshell,
a cockle, or mussel-shell, through
and under the tempestuous seas.
—Reginald Scott,
The Discoverie of Witchcraft

30 Tuesday
1st ♈
Color: Red

Birthday of Zsusanna Budapest,
feminist Witch

31 Wednesday
1st ♈
☽ v/c 8:36 am
☽ enters ♉ 9:21 am
Color: Yellow

Dr. Fian, believed to be the head
of the North Berwick Witches, found
guilty and executed for Witchcraft in
Scotland by personal order of King
James VI (James I of England), 1591

☽ Thursday
1st ♉
☿ enters ♓ 2:13 am
2nd Quarter 9:02 am
Color: Green

2 Friday
2nd ♉
☽ v/c 5:31 am
♀ enters ♈ 2:14 pm
☽ enters ♊ 3:56 pm
Color: Rose

Imbolc
Groundhog Day
Leo Martello becomes a third degree
Welsh traditionalist, 1973

Imbolc

On the eve of Imbolc, prepare your altar for this predawn ritual with nine candles arranged in a circle, facing east to greet the dawn. Choose candles in any color that to you symbolizes the strengthening solar year. Also, try to place your altar where you will actually be able to view the Sun as it rises.

To connect with the energy of the waxing solar year, awaken on Imbolc morning about an hour before dawn. Begin by meditating on the meaning of the waxing year and connecting with its energies. Focus especially on the concept of light being part of the darkness and how, though they are one, the darkness gives birth to the light. Start lighting the candles, one at a time, so that their collective light grows stronger as the first tendrils of sunlight reach over the horizon on this sabbat morning.

—Edain McCoy

---

3 Saturday

2nd ♊
☿ ℞ 8:55 pm
Color: Indigo

Fashion bread dough into dollar signs and bake; serve as a symbolic alter offering for money spells

---

4 Sunday

2nd ♊
☽ v/c 3:12 am
☽ enters ♋ 7:00 pm
Color: Gold

*Imbolc cross-quarter day
(Sun reaches 15° Aquarius)*

February

5 Monday
2nd ♋
Color: White

If you sense danger looming in your future,
use wintergreen as a protection fragrance

6 Tuesday
2nd ♋
☽ v/c 12:30 pm
☿ enters ≈ 2:57 pm
☽ enters ♌ 7:21 pm
Color: Gray

7 Wednesday
2nd ♌
Color: Peach

Death of Thomas Aquinas, scholar who
wrote that heresy was a product of
ignorance and therefore criminal, and
who refuted the *Canon Episcopi*, 1274

☺ Thursday
2nd ♌
Full Moon 2:12 am
☽ v/c 4:25 pm
☽ enters ♍ 6:35 pm
Color: Turquoise

Quickening Moon
Birthday of Susun Weed, owner of
Wise Woman Publishing
Birthday of Evangeline Adams,
American astrologer

9 Friday
3rd ♍
Color: Pink

Quickening Moon

February's Quickening Moon hastens the energy in and around you. Try this Full Moon ritual to make a wish come true:

Assemble the needed tools: a large bowl, one red candle, herbs (basil, cinnamon, clover, ginger, lavender, sage, marjoram, jasmine, black tea), and a wooden spoon, scissors, natural material (cotton, silk, or leather).

Light the red candle, and ask your spirit guides to help you. Place the herbs into the bowl, and crush them with the spoon. A small mound of Wish Quickening Powder will be the end result. Take a pinch of powder and burn as incense while cutting the material into a circle. Place the powder in the center of the circle, gather up the sides, and secure with a strip of material. Take your newly fashioned pouch to a quiet place where water runs, such as a river, stream, or the bath room sink. Open the pouch, pour some powder into your hand, close your eyes, and say: "As I give my wish to you, water make my wish come true." Now, toss the powder into the running water. The water will carry your wish through to fruition.

—Marguerite Elsbeth

---

10 Saturday
3rd ♍
☽ v/c 3:18 pm
☽ enters ♎ 6:46 pm
Color: Blue

Zsusanna Budapest arrested and later convicted for fortunetelling, 1975

---

11 Sunday
3rd ♎
Color: Orange

They dig out all kinds of philtres from everywhere: they search for the agent that arouses mutual love: pills and nails and threads, roots and herbs and shoots, the two-tailed lizard, and charms from mares.
—Apuleius

February

12 Monday
3rd ♎
☽ v/c 12:31 pm
☽ enters ♏ 9:51 pm
Color: Lavender

Gerald Gardner, founder of the
Gardnerian tradition, dies
of heart failure, 1964
Birthday of Cotton Mather, judge in
the Salem Witch Trials, 1668

13 Tuesday
3rd ♏
Color: White

☽ Wednesday
3rd ♏
♂ enters ♐ 3:06 pm
4th Quarter 10:23 pm
☽ v/c 10:23 pm
Color: Brown

Valentine's Day
Elsie Blum, a farmhand from
Oberstedten, Germany, sentenced
to death for Witchcraft, 1652

15 Thursday
4th ♏
☽ enters ♐ 5:02 am
Color: White

Pope Leo X issues bull to ensure that the
secular courts carry out executions of
Witches convicted by the Inquisition,
1521; bull was a response to the courts'
refusal to carry out the work of the Church

16 Friday
4th ♐
Color: Peach

To clear your head, indulge in a cloud of
spearmint aromatherapy while meditating

17 Saturday

4th ♐
☽ v/c 2:22 pm
☽ enters ♑ 3:59 pm
Color: Gray

Prophetic dreams comes to those who sleep
with jasmine tucked under the pillow

18 Sunday

4th ♑
☉ enters ♓ 9:27 am
Color: Yellow

Sun enters Pisces
Celtic Tree Month of Ash begins

Set in Eastern Standard Time (EST)   45

February

19 Monday
4th ♑
☽ v/c 6:03 pm
Color: Gray

Presidents' Day (observed)

20 Tuesday
4th ♑
☽ enters ♒ 4:53 am
Color: Black

Society for Psychical Research,
devoted to paranormal research,
founded in London, 1882

21 Wednesday
4th ♒
Color: White

Stewart Farrar initiated into
Alexandrian Wicca, 1970

Birthday of Patricia Telesco,
Wiccan author

Death of Theodore Parker Mills,
Wiccan elder, 1996

22 Thursday
4th ♒
☽ v/c 7:18 am
☽ enters ♓ 5:45 pm
Color: Violet

Birthday of Sibyl Leek, Wiccan author
Birthday of ShadowCat, Wiccan author

☽ Friday
4th ♓
New Moon 3:21 am
Color: White

Dangerous Chocolate Cake

4 cups cocoa
⅔ cup boiling water
1 cup butter or margarine
2 cups sugar
4 eggs
1 cup milk
1 tbs. vinegar
2½ cups flour
1 tbs. baking soda
½ tsp. salt

Sprinkle 2 tbs. of cocoa in cake pan, and shake until a layer of cocoa covers the bottom. Set pan aside. Mix together flour, baking soda, and salt, and set aside. Mix boiling water in the remaining cocoa. Set aside to cool. Cream the butter or margarine. Add sugar and eggs, one at a time. Stir vinegar into milk, and add to mixture. Blend the flour mixture and the butter mixture alternately. Add the chocolate mix and stir until well blended. Pour into pan. Bake 45 minutes to an hour at 350°. Turn the pan upside down on a cooling rack. Cool for 20 minutes, then gently loosen the cake onto a plate. Sprinkle powdered sugar for decoration.

—Magenta Griffith

24 Saturday
1st ♓
☽ v/c 7:25 pm
Color: Brown

To remove a hex, burn cedar
wood during a liberation spell

25 Sunday
1st ♓
☽ enters ♈ 5:20 am
☿ D 10:42 am
Color: Peach

Black-luggie, hammer-head
Rowan-tree, and red thread
Put the warlocks to their speed.
—Old English charm against Witches

26 Monday
1st ♈
☽ v/c 11:34 pm
Color: Silver

*Halt family conflicts by using
basil when washing your clothes*

27 Tuesday
1st ♈
☽ enters ♉ 3:06 pm
Color: Red

Mardi Gras

28 Wednesday
1st ♉
Color: Yellow

Ash Wednesday

1 Thursday
1st ♉
☽ v/c 1:57 pm
☽ enters ♊ 10:36 pm
Color: Green

Birthday of the Golden Dawn, 1888
Covenant of the Goddess
(COG) formed, 1975
Preliminary hearings in the
Salem Witch Trials held, 1692

◑ Friday
1st ♊
2nd Quarter 9:03 pm
Color: Rose

3 Saturday

2nd ♊
☽ v/c 1:45 pm
Color: Indigo

Listen, O blood, instead of flowing,
instead of pouring forth thy warm stream.
Stop, O blood, like a wall, stop like a
hedge. Stop like a reef in the sea: like
stiff sedge in the moss, like a boulder
in the field, like the pine in the wood.
—Incantation to stop blood flow
from the *Kalevala*

4 Sunday

2nd ♊
☽ enters ♋ 3:24 am
Color: Orange

Church of All Worlds incorporates in
Missouri, 1968, becoming the first Wiccan
church to incorporate in the U.S.

March

5 Monday
2nd ♋
☽ v/c 10:10 pm
Color: Lavender

6 Tuesday
2nd ♋
☽ enters ♌ 5:30 am
Color: White

Birthday of Laurie Cabot, Wiccan author

7 Wednesday
2nd ♌
☽ v/c 10:50 pm
Color: Peach

William Butler Yeats initiated
into the Isis-Urania Temple
of the Golden Dawn, 1890

8 Thursday
2nd ♌
☽ enters ♍ 5:44 am
♀ ℞ 8:06 pm
Color: Turquoise

I wield the large sword of Heaven to
cut down spectres in their five shapes;
one stroke of this divine blade
disperses a myriad of these beings.
—Ancient Chinese spell
inscribed on a sword

☺ Friday
2nd ♍
Full Moon 12:23 pm
☽ v/c 11:01 pm
Color: Pink

Purim
Storm Moon

Set in Eastern Standard Time (EST)

Storm Moon

The Tlingit believe that storms are caused by women who comb their hair outside the house. The Hopi have faith that turning a black stinkbug onto its back will call the rain. March is a generally stormy month, yet these days the weather can be as contrary as Coyote. If the sky is not crying in your area, bring in the spring with this Storm Moon rain ritual:

Obtain a small, round lava rock. Hold the rock in the palm of your right hand (reverse if you are left-handed). Silently call upon the sky, the clouds, and the water spirits to come to your aid. Imagine a gentle rain falling as you begin spinning the lava rock in circles up toward the sky. As you spin the stone, repeat the following chant over and over again:

"Sky, sky, look this way; shed your tears on me this day."

You will know the rite is working when the wind begins to pick up strength. Usually the rain will come, though it may only be a drizzle lasting just a few minutes.

—Marguerite Elsbeth

---

10 Saturday
3rd ♍
☽ enters ♎ 5:47 am
Color: Blue

Dutch clairvoyant and psychic
healer Gerard Croiser born, 1909
Date recorded for first meeting of
Dr. John Dee and Edward Kelly, 1582

---

11 Sunday
3rd ♎
☽ v/c 9:44 pm
Color: Yellow

*To increase one's psychic cognizance
and the ability to recall dreams,
add mugwort to steeping chamomile tea*

March

12 Monday
3rd ♎
☽ enters ♏ 7:43 am
Color: White

Stewart Edward White, psychic researcher, born, 1873; he later became president of the American Society for Psychical Research in San Francisco

13 Tuesday
3rd ♏
Color: Gray

Prior to a handfasting ritual, consecrate the ceremonial venue with salt, water, and purifying incense such as sandalwood or sage

14 Wednesday
3rd ♏
☽ v/c 7:17 am
☽ enters ♐ 1:17 pm
Color: Brown

Jacques de Molay, head of the Knights Templar in France, retracts his confession of heresy before being burned at the stake, 1314

15 Thursday
3rd ♐
Color: White

Pete Pathfinder Davis becomes the first Wiccan priest elected as president of the Interfaith Council of Washington State

◖ Friday
3rd ♐
4th Quarter 3:45 pm
☽ v/c 10:48 pm
☽ enters ♑ 11:02 pm
Color: Peach

Set in Eastern Standard Time (EST)

March

I am the Wind that dances 'cross Earth
I sweep the Winter away with sheer mirth
I waltz through trees, lightly on heel
I promenade through the forest and field
Stirring up dust as I twirl around
Breathing new life into valley and mound
And in my dancing, I whistle a song
The heart joins in and then, before long
I sweep away what is old and used up
Spiritual rubbish and cobwebs and such
Breathing new life right into them, too,
And fresh motivation to all that they do

—Dorothy Morrison

17 Saturday
4th ♑
☿ enters ♓ 1:05 am
♇ ℞ 9:36 pm
Color: Gray

St. Patrick's Day

Eileen J. Garrett born in Ireland, 1893;
she was a founder of the Parapsychology
Foundation, inaugurated in 1951

Eleanor Shaw and Mary Phillips executed
in England for bewitching a woman
and her two children, 1705

18 Sunday
4th ♑
Color: Gold

Celtic Tree Month of Alder begins

Birthday of Edgar Cayce,
psychic researcher

Jacques de Molay retracts his
confession of heresy in public, 1314

March

19 Monday
4th ♑
☽ v/c 9:40 am
☽ enters ♒ 11:36 am
Color: Gray

Elizabethan statute against Witchcraft
enacted, 1563; this statute was replaced in
1604 by a stricter one from King James I

20 Tuesday
4th ♒
☉ enters ♈ 8:31 am
Color: Black

Ostara/Spring Equinox
Sun enters Aries
International Astrology Day

21 Wednesday
4th ♒
☽ v/c 6:03 pm
Color: Brown

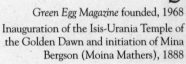

Green Egg Magazine founded, 1968
Inauguration of the Isis-Urania Temple of
the Golden Dawn and initiation of Mina
Bergson (Moina Mathers), 1888
Mandate of Henry VIII against Witchcraft
enacted, 1542; repealed in 1547

22 Thursday
4th ♒
☽ enters ♓ 12:28 am
Color: Violet

Pope Clement urged by Phillip IV
to suppress Templar order, 1311

23 Friday
4th ♓
Color: White

*Accentuate the potency of
a pomander love charm by including
orris root powder as an ingredient*

Ostara

Ostara celebrates the balance of light and dark, with light emerging triumphant, initiating rebirth of the earth and all those creatures and plants who live upon her. From ancient times through the present day, the humble egg has been the enduring symbol of this season for people in almost every culture the world over. To use them in a ritual that honors the earth as the womb of the Goddess, who gives life to all things, decorate hard-boiled eggs in  whatever manner you choose. On the day of the Equinox, take the eggs outside somewhere reasonably private where you can dig into the earth. Gently tap on the earth and tell the Goddess therein that it is time to awaken. With your hands, dig small holes in the ground in which to place the eggs. These serve as an offering to the Goddess and nourishment for her after a long winter's hibernation. It also symbolizes your desire to see life renewed again as summer approaches.

—Edain McCoy

☽ Saturday
4th ♓
☽ v/c 5:58 am
☽ enters ♈ 11:43 am
New Moon 8:21 pm
Color: Brown

Birthday of Alyson Hannigan, who plays Willow on *Buffy the Vampire Slayer*

Arrest of Florence Newton, one of the few Witches burned in Ireland, 1661

25 Sunday
1st ♈
Color: Peach

Innocent III issues bull to establish the Inquisition, 1199

26 Monday

1st ♈
☽ v/c 8:10 am
☽ enters ♉ 8:50 pm
Color: Silver

Birthday of Joseph Campbell, author
and professor of mythology

27 Tuesday

1st ♉
Color: Red

Birthday of Rudolph Steiner,
philosopher and father of the
biodynamic farming movement

28 Wednesday

1st ♉
☽ v/c 11:29 pm
Color: Yellow

Scott Cunningham dies of
complications caused by AIDS, 1993

29 Thursday

1st ♉
☽ enters ♊ 4:01 am
Color: Green

30 Friday

1st ♊
☽ v/c 9:54 pm
Color: Rose

*For an inner healing ritual, invoke the water
nymphs when seeking personal enlightenment*

Colcannon

1 lb. cold boiled potatoes
4 tbs. bacon fat or butter
1 onion, minced
2 cups boiled cabbage, chopped
Salt
Pepper

Mash the potatoes. Fry the onion lightly in the bacon fat (butter may be substituted). Mix potatoes, cabbage, and the onion and season with salt and pepper. Grease a baking dish, pour in the mixture, and bake for thirty minutes in a moderate oven at 350°. If you don't eat it all at one sitting, it makes great potato pancakes the next morning!

—Breid Foxsong

31 Saturday
1st ♊
☽ enters ♋ 9:23 am
Color: Indigo

Last Witch trial in Ireland,
held at Magee Island, 1711
The Fox sisters make "contact" with
the spirit world, sparking the
spiritualist movement, 1848

◑ Sunday
1st ♋
2nd Quarter 5:49 am
Color: Gold

Daylight Saving Time
begins at 2:00 am
April Fool's Day

April

2 Monday

2nd ♋
☽ v/c 9:26 am
☽ enters ♌ 12:54 pm
Color: Silver

*Burn a blend of frankincense and rosemary to
release the spirit of the newly departed*

3 Tuesday

2nd ♌
Color: Red

Thou hast carried thy hands into
the house of eternity, thou art made
perfect in gold, thou dost shine brightly
in sun metal, and thy fingers shine in
the dwelling of Osiris, in the
sanctuary of Horus himself.
—Address to the dead from the
Egyptian Book of the Dead

4 Wednesday

2nd ♌
☽ v/c 11:46 am
☽ enters ♍ 2:46 pm
Color: Peach

5 Thursday

2nd ♍
Color: Turquoise

Trial of Alice Samuel, her
husband, and daughter, who
were accused of bewitching the
wife of Sir Henry Cromwell and
several village children, 1593

6 Friday

2nd ♍
☿ enters ♈ 2:14 am
☽ v/c 1:18 pm
☽ enters ♎ 3:57 pm
Color: Pink

Wind Moon

Round objects with holes in the middle were used by Native American peoples to call the wind. They believed that the wind called the Moon and carried the voices of the people to her. Use this ritual to call the Wind Moon:

Just before Moonrise, have ready a two-holed, one inch white button and a length of red embroidery thread. Wrap the thread once around your elbow to form a loop. Cut any remaining thread. Place one end of thread through each hole in the button. Tie the loose thread ends into a knot. Hold the loop of thread so that the button hangs between the two ends. Flip the button round and round until the thread is tightly twisted. Now, pull your fingers away from each other, and continue doing so with an in and out motion (like one would use when playing an accordion) until the button begins to hum a natural wind song that will bring about a breeze. When you feel the breeze, ask the wind to call up the Moon. As the Moon rises, ask the wind to carry your prayers to her.

—Marguerite Elsbeth

☺ Saturday

2nd ♎
☿ ℞ 1:02 pm
Full Moon 10:22 pm
Color: Blue

Wind Moon
Church of all Worlds founded, 1962
First Wiccan "tract" published
by Pete Pathfinder Davis, 1996

---

8 Sunday

3rd ♎
☽ v/c 7:31 am
☽ enters ♏ 6:01 pm
Color: Orange

Palm Sunday
Passover begins
William Alexander Aynton initiated into
the Isis-Urania temple of the Golden
Dawn, 1896; he would later be called the
"Grand Old Man" of the Golden Dawn

April

9 Monday
3rd ♏
Color: White

10 Tuesday
3rd ♏
☽ v/c 8:43 pm
☽ enters ♐ 10:47 pm
Color: Gray

Birthday of Rev. Montague Summers, orthodox scholar and author of *A History of Witchcraft and Demonology*, 1880; despite living in relatively modern times, Summers believed that Witchcraft (as defined by the Inquisition, not Wicca) was real and admired the work of the authors of the *Malleus Maleficarum*

11 Wednesday
3rd ♐
Color: White

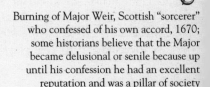

Burning of Major Weir, Scottish "sorcerer" who confessed of his own accord, 1670; some historians believe that the Major became delusional or senile because up until his confession he had an excellent reputation and was a pillar of society

12 Thursday
3rd ♐
☽ v/c 8:56 pm
Color: Violet

Handfasting of Oberon and Morning Glory Zell, 1974

13 Friday
3rd ♐
☽ enters ♑ 7:21 am
Color: Pea

First confession of Witchcraft by Isobel Gowdie, whose case is considered unusual because no torture was used to extract her confession, Scotland, 1662

Set in Eastern Standard Time (EST)

April

I am the Rain, the Bringer of Life
I bring the moisture and ease all strife
I soothe the Earth—I quench Her thirst
I nudge seeds gently awake so they burst
Into full germination so they can sprout
I cleanse the Earth within and without
But that isn't all; I give so much more
I cleanse the spirit from aura to core
I inspire and unblock creativity flow
And bring physical energy to all I know
Mine is true happiness and pure delight
I bring the rainbow back in the Light

—Dorothy Morrison

---

14 Saturday
3rd ♑
Color: Brown

Passover ends
Adoption of the Principles of
Wiccan Belief at "Witch Meet"
in St. Paul, Minnesota, 1974

☽ Sunday
3rd ♑
4th Quarter 10:31 am
☽ v/c 6:00 pm
☽ enters ♒ 7:11 pm
Color: Yellow

Easter
Celtic Tree Month of Willow begins
Birthday of Elizabeth Montgomery,
who played Samantha on *Bewitched*

April

16 Monday
4th ≈
Color: Gray

Birthday of Margot Adler, author
of *Drawing Down the Moon*

17 Tuesday
4th ≈
Color: Black

Aleister Crowley breaks into
and takes over the Golden
Dawn temple, providing the
catalyst for the demise of the
original Golden Dawn, 1900

18 Wednesday
4th ≈
☽ v/c 7:26 am
☽ enters ♓ 8:00 am
Color: Brown

19 Thursday
4th ♓
☉ enters ♉ 7:36 pm
♀ D 11:34 pm
Color: White

Sun enters Taurus
Conviction of Witches at
second of four famous trials at
Chelmsford, England, 1579

20 Friday
4th ♓
☽ v/c 12:40 pm
♄ enters ♊ 4:59 pm
☽ enters ♈ 7:18 pm
Color: Peach

To express gratitude to the Earth Mother,
serve sweet peas during a gardening ritual

Set in Eastern Standard Time (EST)

21 Saturday

4th ♈
☿ enters ♉ 3:08 pm
Color: Gray

22 Sunday

4th ♈
☽ v/c 10:34 pm
Color: Peach

Earth Day; the first Earth Day was in 1970

April

☽ **Monday**
4th ♈
☽ enters ♉ 3:56 am
New Moon 10:26 am
Color: Lavender

Edward III of England begins the
Order of the Garter, which Margaret
Murray later links to Witchcraft, 1350

First National All-Woman Conference on
Women's Spirituality held, Boston, 1976

---

24 Tuesday
1st ♉
Color: Gray

---

25 Wednesday
1st ♉
☽ v/c 12:08 am
☽ enters ♊ 10:11 am
Color: Yellow

USA Today reports that Patricia
Hutchins is the first military
Wiccan granted religious leave
for the sabbats, 1989

---

26 Thursday
1st ♊
Color: Green

*Be certain to let your hair flow loose during
ritual work to enhance the power of the act*

---

27 Friday
1st ♊
☽ v/c 11:12 am
☽ enters ♋ 2:49 pm
Color: Rose

They bewitch all men, whoso shall
come to them, whoso draws nigh them
unwittingly and hears the sound of the
Sirens' voice, never doth he see wife or
babes on his return; but the Sirens
enchant him with their clear song.
—Homer

Oat Flour Banana Bread

⅓ cup margarine
⅔ cup sugar
2 eggs
2 cups oat flour
2 tsp. baking soda
½ tsp. salt
1 cup very ripe bananas (2 large or 3 small), mashed
½ cup nuts, chopped nuts

Grease a 9 x 5 loaf pan. Cream the margarine, add the sugar and mix well. Add the eggs one at a time, beating well after each one. Add the dry ingredients, blend in, then add the bananas. Stir in nuts. Pour in the greased pan. Bake at 350° for 1 hour or until a toothpick comes out clean. Cool before cutting, or it will crumble. This is a good recipe to take to potlucks where there will be people sensitive to wheat.

—Magenta Griffith

28 Saturday

1st ♋
☽ v/c 4:53 pm
Color: Indigo

29 Sunday

1st ♋
☽ enters ♌ 6:25 pm
Color: Gold

Birthday of Ed Fitch, Wiccan author

☽ Monday

1st ♌
2nd Quarter 12:08 pm
Color: Silver

Walpurgis Night; traditionally the
German Witches gather on the Blocksberg,
a mountain in northeastern Germany

Alex Sanders, founder of the
Alexandrian Tradition of Witchcraft,
dies of lung cancer, 1988

1 Tuesday

2nd ♌
☽ v/c 6:43 pm
☽ enters ♍ 9:16 pm
Color: Black

Beltane/May Day

Order of the Illuminati, an organization
dedicated to ceremonial magic, formed in
Bavaria by Adam Weishaupt, 1776

Death of Arnold Crowther, stage
magician and Gardnerian Witch, 1974

2 Wednesday

2nd ♍
Color: Brown

3 Thursday

2nd ♍
☽ v/c 9:39 pm
☽ enters ♎ 11:50 pm
Color: White

Birthday of D. J. Conway, Wiccan author

Edward Kelly tries to convince Dr.
John Dee and their wives to sign a
"wife swapping" document, supposedly
at the insistence of a spirit named
Madini; the wives and Dee are not
thrilled with the arrangement;
no record of the results, 1587

4 Friday

2nd ♎
Color: Pink

The *New York Herald Tribune*
carries the story of a woman who
brought her neighbor to court on
a charge of bewitchment, 1895

Beltane

Beltane honors the sacred marriage of the God and Goddess, whose union will produce the harvests to come. It also celebrates the start of summer in full bloom. For this ritual, gather or purchase wildflowers. With raffia, twine, or string, tie the flowers together in long garlands; ten feet in length or longer is perfect. These don't have to look professionally crafted. They only need to hold together for the purposes of your ritual. When you

have completed the garlands, go out to a park or wooded area. Touch the land and its plants and trees with your hands, allowing yourself to connect with the pulsing lifeforce of the area. Look around for items that are either feminine or masculine in their energy and begin linking them together with the flowery garlands to honor the union of the divine male and female energies. For example, you can link stones to oak trees, riverbanks to abandoned fire pits, or flowering plants to spiky ones.

—Edain McCoy

---

5 Saturday

2nd ♎
☿ enters ♊ 11:53 pm
Color: Gray

Cinco de Mayo
Beltane cross-quarter day
(Sun reaches 15° Taurus)

---

6 Sunday

2nd ♎
☽ v/c 1:03 am
☽ enters ♏ 3:00 am
Color: Yellow

Long Island Church of Aphrodite
formed by Reverend Gleb Botkin, 1938

☺ Monday
2nd ♏
Full Moon 8:53 am
☽ v/c 10:25 pm
Color: White

Flower Moon

8 Tuesday
3rd ♏
☽ enters ♐ 8:05 am
Color: Gray

At the time of a waning moon,
perform a ritual to aid in losing weight

9 Wednesday
3rd ♐
Color: Peach

Joan of Arc canonized, 1920
First day of the Lemuria, a Roman
festival of the dead; this festival
was probably borrowed from the
Etruscans and is one possible
ancestor of our modern Halloween

10 Thursday
3rd ♐
☽ v/c 2:20 pm
☽ enters ♑ 4:10 pm
♆ ℞ 8:13 pm
Color: Violet

11 Friday
3rd ♑
♂ ℞ 11:08 am
Color: White

Massachusetts Bay Colony Puritans
ban Christmas celebrations
because they are too Pagan, 1659

Flower Moon

Bring May flowers into your life, and increase your natural beauty with this Flower Moon rite:

Gather up a plate of rich topsoil, a small flower pot, your favorite flower seeds, one green candle, a full-sized mirror, and a floral-scented essential oil. Sit in front of the mirror. Rub the oil into the candle, and plant it firmly in the dish of soil. Light the candle, keeping it between you and the mirror. Look deeply into the eyes of your reflection. What is beautiful about you? Consider only your most attractive physical, emotional, mental, and spiritual qualities, then blow out the candle. Repeat this ritual every night until the candle has burned down.

Remove the wax from the soil and bury it outdoors, in the earth, and with it all your less-than-lovely characteristics. Now, put the soil from the plate into the flower pot, along with the seeds. Give the flowers you have planted lots of love and attention, imbuing them with all the beautiful qualities you have noticed about yourself. As the flowers grow in beauty, so will you!

—Marguerite Elsbeth

---

12 Saturday
3rd ♑
☽ v/c 11:17 am
Color: Blue

To consecrate a new wand,
invoke the salamanders for sanctification

---

13 Sunday
3rd ♑
☽ enters ♒ 3:20 am
Color: Orange

Mother's Day
Celtic Tree Month of Hawthorn begins

May

14 Monday
3rd ≈
Color: Lavender

Widow Robinson of Kidderminster
and her two daughters are arrested for
trying to prevent the return of Charles II
from exile by use of magic, 1660

☽ Tuesday
3rd ≈
4th Quarter 5:11 am
☽ v/c 1:53 pm
☽ enters ♓ 4:01 pm
Color: Red

16 Wednesday
4th ♓
Color: Yellow

Each month there is a spirit that goes
forth and walks by night; These spirits
that walk by night must be appeased;
For the external influences act on man,
in accordance with the stars.
—Kwang-Tchu,
Treatise on Wandering Influences

17 Thursday
4th ♓
Color: Green

*To add might to a fertility ritual,
include a sprig of hawthorne*

18 Friday
4th ♓
☽ v/c 1:18 am
☽ enters ♈ 3:41 am
Color: Peach

Set in Eastern Standard Time (EST)

19 Saturday
4th ♈
Color: Indigo

20 Sunday
4th ♈
☽ v/c 9:48 am
☽ enters ♉ 12:29 pm
☉ enters ♊ 6:44 pm
Color: Gold

Sun enters Gemini

May

21 Monday
4th ♉
Color: Gray

Birthday of Gwyddion Pendderwen,
Pagan bard, 1946

☽ Tuesday
4th ♉
☽ v/c 9:06 am
☽ enters ♊ 6:12 pm
New Moon 9:46 pm
Color: White

Adoption of the Earth Religion
Anti-Abuse Act, 1988

23 Wednesday
1st ♊
Color: Brown

24 Thursday
1st ♊
☽ v/c 6:12 pm
☽ enters ♋ 9:42 pm
Color: Turquoise

They are called scryers who by divining
in bright and polished objects—
such as gleaming swords, basins,
cups, and various kinds of mirrors—
satisfy the consultations of inquirers.
—John of Salisbury

25 Friday
1st ♋
Color: Brown

Date given as the day Dr. John
Dee began crystal-gazing, 1581

Scott Cunningham initiated into
the Traditional Gwyddonic
Order of the Wicca, 1981

Tortellini Summer Salad

1 tsp. shredded lemon peel
3 tbs. lemon juice
1 tsp. Dijon mustard
½ tsp. sugar
¼ tsp. salt
1 clove minced garlic
2 9-oz. pkgs. refrigerated cheese tortellini
½ lb. asparagus spears, chopped
½ lb. broccoli tops, chopped
1 yellow and 1 red pepper (sweet)
2 tbs. olive oil
4 green onions, sliced

In screw-top jar combine first six ingredients. Cover; shake well. Refrigerate. In a large saucepan, cook tortellini according to package directions, adding chopped vegetables in the last minute of cooking time. Drain and rinse. Toss tortellini-vegetable mix with olive oil. Cover and refrigerate for 2 to 24 hours. Before serving, stir in onions, and add ½ cup Parmesan cheese if desired. Shake dressing, pour over all, toss lightly to coat.

—Breid Foxsong

26 Saturday

1st ♋
☽ v/c 7:44 am
Color: Blue

Summon the tempest spirits when a loved one passes, to serve as guides for the soul

27 Sunday

1st ♋
☽ enters ♌ 12:12 am
Color: Peach

Birthday of Morning Glory
Zell, Church of All Worlds
Final confession of Witchcraft by
Isobel Gowdie, Scotland, 1662

28 Monday
1st ♌
Color: Silver

Memorial Day (observed)
Shavuot

◐ Tuesday
1st ♌
☽ v/c 12:13 am
☽ enters ♍ 2:38 am
♅ R 10:11 am
2nd Quarter 5:09 pm
Color: Black

*To enhance your intellect, call
upon the sylphs of the air; give
thanks for the consciousness of breath*

30 Wednesday
2nd ♍
Color: Yellow

Death of Joan of Arc, 1431

31 Thursday
2nd ♍
☽ v/c 4:40 am
☽ enters ♎ 5:41 am
Color: White

Witchcraft celebrates
pale Hecate's offerings
—Shakespeare, *Macbeth*

1 Friday
2nd ♎
Color: Rose

Witchcraft Act of 1563
takes effect in England

2 Saturday

2nd ♎
☽ v/c 9:41 am
☽ enters ♏ 9:56 am
Color: Blue

Birthday of Alessandro
di Cagliostro, magician, 1743

3 Sunday

2nd ♏
Color: Gold

June

4 Monday

2nd ♏
☿ R 12:21 am
☽ v/c 6:29 am
☽ enters ♐ 3:58 pm
Color: Silver

To purify yourself of negative patterns, burn a fire of birch twigs

☺ Tuesday

2nd ♐
Full Moon 8:39 pm
Color: Red

Strong Sun Moon

6 Wednesday

3rd ♐
♀ enters ♉ 5:25 am
☽ v/c 11:41 pm
Color: Peach

7 Thursday

3rd ♐
☽ enters ♑ 12:23 am
☽ v/c 1:57 am
Color: Turquoise

*Take the oak rod, turn in the direction in which you want to fly, and write the name of your destination on the ground.
—Method of flight from the Key of Solomon*

8 Friday

3rd ♑
Color: Pink

Strong Sun Moon

June's Strong Sun Moon ritual will help you to regenerate your body, mind, and soul:

Lie on the earth, or indoors in a comfortable place. Become aware of the gravity pulling your body down like a magnet, while simultaneously feeling the Sun's heat filling you with fiery energy from above. When you feel that your body is filled to overflowing with vital force, sit or stand up. Use your powers of imagination to step out of your body and face yourself. Reaching forward with "spirit" hands, begin to shape and mold your body into the spirit you feel you truly are. You may become whatever creature or thing that best exemplifies your self-image—Celtic goddess, an Indian warrior, or an animal form. Remember to include all the qualities of the spirit you are taking on—physical, emotional, mental, and spiritual. When you are finished, mentally have your spirit-self step back into your new spirit body. Now, dance your new spirit under the Strong Sun Moon. Howl, sing, soar, jump, or buck. Dance until your spirit body is finished dancing.

—Marguerite Elsbeth

---

9 Saturday

3rd ♑
☽ enters ♒ 11:20 am
Color: Indigo

Birthday of Grace Cook, medium and
founder of the White Eagle Lodge

---

10 Sunday

3rd ♒
Color: Orange

Celtic Tree Month of Oak begins
Hanging of Bridget Bishop, first to
die in the Salem Witch Trials, 1692

June

11 Monday
3rd ≈
☽ v/c 7:38 pm
☽ enters ♓ 11:53 pm
Color: White

James I Witchcraft Statute replaces the
1563 mandate with stricter penalties, 1604

12 Tuesday
3rd ♓
Color: Black

○ Wednesday
3rd ♓
4th Quarter 10:28 pm
Color: White

Birthday of Gerald Gardner, founder of
the Gardnerian Tradition

Richard of Gloucester tries to usurp the
English throne by declaring that the
widow of Edward IV (the previous king)
had bewitched the king and that she
colluded with the king's mistress, Jane
Shore, to cripple Gloucester, 1483

14 Thursday
4th ♓
☽ v/c 5:26 am
☽ enters ♈ 12:03 pm
Color: Violet

Flag Day

15 Friday
4th ♈
Color: Peach

Margaret Jones becomes the first person
executed as a Witch in the Massachusetts
Bay Colony, 1648; She was a Boston
doctor who was accused of Witchcraft
when several of her patients died

June

Mine is the Summer, for I am the Sun
I glimmer and shine until day is done
I bring the warmth and I bring the light
And victory, energy, health, and delight
All that I touch grows lush and thrives
For I bring abundance into all lives
I touch the heart and the spirit as well
Bringing them joy while under My spell
But even with that, I sharpen the mind
I clear the path of problems that bind
I bring solutions and I ease all stress
For I am the Sun, and I bring success

       —Dorothy Morrison

---

16 Saturday

4th ♈
☽ v/c 1:32 pm
☽ enters ♉ 9:39 pm
Color: Gray

Wear pennyroyal garlands
to relieve tension headaches

---

17 Sunday
4th ♉
Color: Yellow

Father's Day
Birthday of Starhawk, Wiccan author

June

18 Monday
4th ♉
☽ v/c 6:21 pm
Color: Lavender

Church of All Worlds
chartered with the IRS, 1970

19 Tuesday
4th ♉
☽ enters ♊ 3:42 am
Color: Gray

Birthday of James I of England,
famous for his anti-Witchcraft laws

Marriage of Margot Adler in the
first Wiccan handfasting to be carried in
the *New York Times* society pages, 1988

20 Wednesday
4th ♊
☽ v/c 10:24 pm
Color: Brown

*At a New Moon ritual, pay
homage to Artemis, the Huntress,
with a feast of wild game*

☽ Thursday
4th ♊
☉ enters ♋ 2:38 am
☽ enters ♋ 6:40 am
New Moon 6:58 am
Color: White

Midsummer/Litha/Summer Solstice
Sun enters Cancer
Solar eclipse 7:05 am, 0° ♋ 10'

22 Friday
1st ♋
☽ v/c 9:11 am
Color: Rose

Final Witchcraft law in
England repealed, 1951

Litha

Litha is the Midsummer celebration of the Sun at its zenith. It is a time when heat, light, and the Sun-God himself are at their strongest. After this brief moment in time, their strength will start to diminish as the year wanes gradually to darkness. For this ritual you will need a small amount of dried herbs, a fire- and heat-proof container in which to burn them, and some matches. Use caution, so that you don't start a fire outdoors or set off  your smoke detector indoors. Choose herbs that share an affinity with the Sun and fire such as bay leaves, sunflowers, basil, frankincense, or any mint plant. Verbally pay homage to the Sun-God, then light the herbs. They will burn fast and hot—and may not smell wonderful! Revel in the heat and light pouring from the container and feel the way it symbolizes the quick apex and descent of the Sun on Litha.

—Edain McCoy

23 Saturday
1st ♋
☽ enters ♌ 7:55 am
Color: Brown

24 Sunday
1st ♌
Color: Peach

Birthday of Janet Farrar, Wiccan author
James I Witchcraft Statute of 1604 is replaced in 1763 with a law against pretending to practice divination and Witchcraft; law stands until 1951

June/July

25 Monday

1st ♌
☽ v/c 2:22 am
☽ enters ♍ 8:57 am
Color: Gray

A law is introduced in Germany by
Archbishop Siegfried III to encourage
conversion rather than burning of
heretics, 1233; law is a response to the
fanatical Witch persecutions by Conrad of
Marbug, who answers the new law by
persecuting nobles, where in the past
his target had been the poor

26 Tuesday

1st ♍
Color: White

Birthday of Stewart Farrar, Wiccan author
Richard of Gloucester assumes the English
throne after accusing the widowed
queen of Edward IV of Witchcraft

○ Wednesday

1st ♍
☽ v/c 5:12 am
☽ enters ♎ 11:11 am
2nd Quarter 10:19 pm
Color: Yellow

Birthday of Scott Cunningham,
Wiccan author

28 Thursday

2nd ♎
☿ D 12:48 am
Color: Green

29 Friday

2nd ♎
☽ v/c 10:07 am
☽ enters ♏ 3:28 pm
Color: Pink

She undertakes by her incantations
to give peace to minds at will, or
to fill them with heavy cares; to
arrest the flow of rivers and turn back
the stars in their course: she summons
the nocturnal spirits: you will see the
ground rumble beneath her feet.
—Virgil, speaking of a temple priestess

Gazpacho

6 cups tomato juice (1 46-oz. can)
1 tbs. honey (optional)
2–3 cloves garlic, finely minced
3 tbs. lemon juice
¼ cup olive oil
1 tsp. soy sauce (to taste)
1 cucumber, finely chopped
1 cup carrots, shredded
1 cup celery, finely chopped
1 green pepper, finely chopped
¼ cup green onion or chives, chopped
2 large tomatoes, chopped

Combine liquids and mix until blended. Add vegetables. Chill overnight or at least a few hours. Feel free to experiment with how coarsely or finely you chop or shred vegetables. A food processor helps, but it will turn some things into a puree, and the texture differences are part of the delight.

—Steven Posch

---

30 Saturday
2nd ♏
Color: Indigo

Throw a white agate into
a natural body of water when
wishcrafting for something truly fanciful

---

1 Sunday
2nd ♏
☽ v/c 2:25 pm
☽ enters ♐ 10:13 pm
Color: Gold

---

2 Monday
2nd ♐
Color: Silver

Take a bath with your lover; add orange blossom oil to the water to add constancy and dedication to your union

3 Tuesday
2nd ♐
Color: Red

Trial of Joan Prentice, who was accused of sending an imp in the form of a ferret to bite children; she allegedly had two imps named Jack and Jill, 1549

4 Wednesday
2nd ♐
☽ v/c 3:36 am
☽ enters ♑ 7:21 am
Color: Peach

Independence Day

☺ Thursday
2nd ♑
Full Moon 10:04 am
☽ v/c 10:04 am
♀ enters ♊ 11:44 am
Color: Turquoise

Lunar eclipse 13° ♑ 39', 9:56 am
Blessing Moon
Conviction of Witches at third of four famous trials at Chelmsford, England, 1589

6 Friday
3rd ♑
☽ enters ♒ 6:33 pm
Color: Pink

Scott Cunningham is initiated into the Ancient Pictish Gaelic Way, 1981

Blessing Moon

Blessings are living energies. Sharing your many blessings has far-reaching effects—feelings of peace, love, and happiness are instantly returned to you. This Blessing Moon ritual is a way to demonstrate your gratitude and pass healing from one person, place, or thing to another, so all may blessed be. Perform the following ritual at moonrise either in or out of doors:

Stand, facing east. Moving clockwise, draw a magic circle all around you. Well up feelings of gratitude in your heart. Now, raise your arms above you, and with palms open, bless the sky. Lower your arms toward the ground, blessing Mother Earth, the animals, plants, minerals, and elementals. While extending your arms before you in blessing for the gifts you receive, feel grateful that everything you want and need is yours now. Again, moving clockwise, turn right to bless your friends and loved ones. Acknowledge the place of memories behind you, forgiving and blessing all your past experiences. Turn right again, blessing all who have caused you pain. Return to your original position, and thank the Blessing Moon for shining her light upon you.

—Marguerite Elsbeth

---

7 Saturday
3rd ≈
Color: Blue

---

8 Sunday
3rd ≈
Color: Orange

Celtic Tree Month of Holly begins

July

9 Monday
3rd ≈
☽ v/c 5:28 am
☽ enters ♓ 7:05 am
Color: White

Birthday of Amber K, Wiccan author

Death of Herman Slater,
proprietor of Magickal Childe
bookstore in New York, 1992

10 Tuesday
3rd ♓
Color: Black

11 Wednesday
3rd ♓
☽ v/c 7:09 pm
☽ enters ♈ 7:36 pm
Color: White

They (Witches) hear a thunderous noise
at night of their mistress as she passes
with her retinue of dancing spirits;
and only then are they wont to anoint
themselves so they may be bourne
through the air and follow until they
all come to the assigned spot.
—Bartolomeus Spina, *Quaestio de strigbus*

12 Thursday
3rd ♈
☿ enters ♋ 5:47 pm
♃ enters ♋ 7:02 pm
Color: Violet

*Burn mugwort incense in your
bedchamber to inspire dream recollections*

◖ Friday
3rd ♈
4th Quarter 1:45 pm
☽ v/c 6:52 pm
Color: Peach

Birthday of Dr. John Dee, magician

Birthday of Dr. Margaret Murray,
Egyptologist

July

I am the harbinger of true Liberty
I'm in the vines that grow wild and free
I'm in the animals roaming the Earth
Running in joy and playing in mirth
I am the whole of everything brave
I fulfill anything that you might crave
I am boundless and endless in my energy
For my gifts are freedom and fertility
But My valued gifts and all they can be
Come not without paying a reasonable fee
Of liable action for that said and done
As you enjoy living free 'neath the Sun
—Dorothy Morrison

---

14 Saturday
4th ♈
☽ enters ♉ 6:13 am
Color: Gray

First crop circles recorded
on Silbury Hill, 1988

---

15 Sunday
4th ♉
Color: Yellow

July

16 Monday
4th ♉
☽ v/c 2:41 am
☽ enters ♊ 1:26 pm
Color: Lavender

For a glamour to illuminate your hair, combine orris root, pansies, and parsley in magically charged water

17 Tuesday
4th ♊
Color: Gray

First airing of *The Witching Hour*, a Pagan radio show hosted by Winter Wren and Don Lewis, on station WONX in Evanston, Illinois, 1992

18 Wednesday
4th ♊
☽ v/c 6:46 am
☽ enters ♋ 4:56 pm
Color: Brown

19 Thursday
4th ♋
♂ D 5:45 pm
Color: White

Rebecca Nurse hanged in Salem, Massachusetts, 1692

☽ Friday
4th ♋
New Moon 2:44 pm
☽ v/c 2:44 pm
☽ enters ♌ 5:43 pm
Color: Rose

Pope Adrian VI issues a bull to the Inquisition to re-emphasize the 1503 bull of Julius II calling for the purging of "sorcerers by fire and sword," 1523

Lord Hunterford of England executed for treason for consulting Mother Roche, a Witch, and speculating on the king's death, 1540

21 Saturday
1st ♌
Color: Brown

22 Sunday
1st ♌
☽ v/c 7:34 am
☉ enters ♌ 1:26 pm
☽ enters ♍ 5:29 pm
Color: Peach

Sun enters Leo
Northamptonshire Witches
condemned, 1612
First modern recorded sighting
of the Loch Ness Monster, 1930

July

23 Monday
1st ♍
Color: Gray

Carry a sprig of alfalfa in a money mojo bag to promote fiscal health and security

24 Tuesday
1st ♍
☽ v/c 2:48 am
☽ enters ♎ 6:08 pm
Color: White

Letter from Johannes Junius, a German accused of Witchcraft, to his daughter Veronica dated July 24, 1628; in the letter, one of the few to survive from that time, Junius details his torture and trial, and begs his daughter to keep the letter secret so that the people who smuggled it out of the jail for him would not be beheaded

25 Wednesday
1st ♎
Color: Yellow

Death of Pope Innocent VIII, who issued bull *Summis Desiderantes Affectibus*, 1492

26 Thursday
1st ♎
☽ v/c 10:10 am
☽ enters ♏ 9:17 pm
Color: Violet

Confession of Chelmsford Witches at first of four famous trials at Chelmsford, 1566; the others were held in 1579, 1589, and 1645; "Witch Finder General" Matthew Hopkins presided at the 1645 trials

○ Friday
1st ♏
2nd Quarter 5:08 am
Color: Green

Jennet Preston becomes the first of the "Malkin Tower" Witches to be hung; she was convicted of hiring Witches to help her murder Thomas Lister, 1612

Set in Eastern Standard Time (EST)

Dandelion Muffins

2 cups flour
1 tbs. baking powder
½ tsp. salt
3 tbs. sugar
1 egg, well beaten
1 cup milk
3 tbs. oil
½ cup dandelion petals
1 tsp. nutmeg
2 tbs. sugar

Combine the flour, baking powder, salt, and 3 tbs. sugar and mix well. In a separate bowl, combine egg, milk, and oil. Add to dry ingredients and stir gently. Using your fingers, break apart dandelion petals until fine, and mix with nutmeg and 2 tbs. sugar. Stir into batter. Finish stirring batter until the dry ingredients are moist but still lumpy. Spoon batter into greased muffin pans, filling pans only ⅔ full. Bake at 425° for 20 to 28 minutes, depending on size of muffins. Makes about 18 medium muffins. These are great for the cakes-and-wine part of a ritual, or any other special occasion.

—Kirin Lee

---

28 Saturday

2nd ♏
☽ v/c 10:50 pm
Color: Indigo

---

29 Sunday

2nd ♏
☽ enters ♐ 3:44 am
Color: Gold

Agnes Waterhouse, one of the Chelmsford Witches, is hanged under the new Witchcraft statute of Elizabeth I, 1566; she was accused of having a spotted cat familiar named Sathan

---

July/August

30 Monday
2nd ♐
☿ enters ♌ 5:18 am
Color: Silver

Conrad of Marburg is murdered on the open road, presumably because he had shifted from persecuting poor heretics to nobles, 1233; in the same year Marburg's report on heretics prompts Pope Gregory IX to issue *Vox in Rama*, a bull accusing them of orgies, devil worship, and cannibalism

31 Tuesday
2nd ♐
☽ v/c 11:24 am
☽ enters ♑ 1:16 pm
☽ v/c 9:21 pm
Color: Red

Date of fabled meeting of British Witches to raise cone of power to stop Hitler's invasion of England, 1940

Birthday of H. P. Blavatsky, founder of the Theosophical Society

Birthday of Ellen Evert Hopman, Wiccan author

1 Wednesday
2nd ♑
♀ enters ♋ 7:18 am
Color: Peach

Lammas/Lughnasadh

Birthday of Edward Kelly, medium of Dr. John Dee, 1555

Discovery of Lindow Man, 1984; Lindow Man has been dated to the second century BC and is believed to be a Druid

2 Thursday
2nd ♑
Color: Turquoise

Birthday of Henry Steele Olcott, who cofounded the Theosophical Society with H. P. Blavatsky

3 Friday
2nd ♑
☽ enters ♒ 12:53 am
Color: Pink

Lammas

For this ritual celebrating the harvesting of grains, you will need only a loaf of bread. Go to a secluded river bank or a private section of land and get comfortable on the ground. Divide the bread into three equal parts. Slowly begin eating the first part, savoring its taste and texture while focusing on the Earth Goddess who gave you this gift that is often called the "staff of life." When you are done, scatter the second third over the land near you as an offering back to her that she may share with the creatures who walk her face. Hold the last part of the bread between your hands and think about how the year is waning, heat and light losing strength every day. Project into the bread something you want to be rid of, such as a bad habit or thought pattern. Tear the bread into small pieces and cast them away from you into the flowing river or bury them in the soft earth.

—Edain McCoy

☺ **Saturday**

2nd ≈
Full Moon 12:56 am
☽ v/c 11:52 pm
Color: Blue

Corn Moon

---

5 Sunday

3rd ≈
☽ enters ⟩⟨ 1:30 pm
Color: Orange

Celtic Tree Month of Hazel begins

August

6 Monday
3rd ♓
Color: White

Lammas cross-quarter day
(Sun reaches 15° Leo)

7 Tuesday
3rd ♓
☽ v/c 12:39 am
Color: Black

Now she holds the crowd of
infernal spirits by her magic howl.
—Tibullus, writing about a Witch

8 Wednesday
3rd ♓
☽ enters ♈ 2:05 am
Color: White

If you hope to avoid a quarrel,
dab yourself with basil oil

9 Thursday
3rd ♈
☽ v/c 11:53 pm
Color: Violet

10 Friday
3rd ♈
☽ enters ♉ 1:23 pm
Color: Peach

Use cinnamon, ginger, and multicolored
carnations in a vitality bath splash
formulated to unlock personal fortitude
and enhance magical potency

Set in Eastern Standard Time (EST)

Corn Moon

Corn symbolizes fruitfulness and abundance. Try this Corn Moon ritual to offer thanksgiving and increase your prosperity:

You will need a ripe ear of corn, a needle, yellow embroidery thread, and a small bowl of corn meal. Go outdoors and find a tree with lower branches within easy reach. Sit for a moment, envisioning what it is that will make you feel prosperous. Cradle the ear of corn in your arms as if it were a child, impressing it with your vision. Carefully remove thirteen corn kernels from the ear. While sewing a length of thread through each kernel, say: "Corn Mother, let not the cold return so soon; share your golden fruits this Moon." Hang the kernels from the branches of the tree, bury what remains beneath it, and then sprinkle the corn meal clockwise around the trunk. Ask the birds to take your offerings to Corn Mother, and offer up a prayer for abundance.

—Marguerite Elsbeth

11 Saturday

3rd ♉
Color: Gray

Laurie Cabot withdraws from Salem, Massachusetts, mayoral race, 1987

◑ Sunday

3rd ♉
4th Quarter 2:53 am
☽ v/c 5:32 pm
☽ enters ♊ 9:59 pm
Color: Yellow

August

13 Monday
4th ♊
Color: Lavender

Aradia de Toscano allegedly
born in Volterra, Italy, 1313

Church of Wicca founded in Australia
by Lady Tamara Von Forslun, 1989

14 Tuesday
4th ♊
☿ enters ♍ 12:04 am
☽ v/c 2:42 pm
Color: Gray

15 Wednesday
4th ♊
☽ enters ♋ 2:55 am
Color: Brown

Birthday of Charles Godfrey Leland,
author of *Aradia, Gospel of Witches*, 1824

16 Thursday
4th ♋
☽ v/c 8:03 am
Color: White

*For a harmonious gathering, create a floral
table setting with lilies of the valley*

17 Friday
4th ♋
☽ enters ♌ 4:25 am
Color: Rose

Scott Cunningham's first
initiation into Wicca, 1973

Set in Eastern Standard Time (EST)

☽ **Saturday**

4th ♌

New Moon 9:55 pm

☽ v/c 9:55 pm

Color: Brown

Father Urbain Grandier found
guilty of bewitching nuns at a
convent in Loudoun, France, 1634

19 Sunday

1st ♌

☽ enters ♍ 3:53 am

Color: Peach

John Willard and Reverend
George Burroughs put to death
in the Salem Witch Trials, 1692

August

20 Monday
1st ♍
☽ v/c 3:21 pm
Color: Gray

Execution of Lancashire Witches, 1612
Birthday of Ann Moura, Wiccan author
Birthday of H. P. Lovecraft, horror
writer and alleged magician

21 Tuesday
1st ♍
☽ enters ♎ 3:19 am
Color: White

22 Wednesday
1st ♎
☉ enters ♍ 8:27 pm
☽ v/c 8:34 pm
Color: Yellow

Sun enters Virgo
Order of the Rosy Cross established, 1623
Pope John XXII, one of the first
popes to promote the theory that
Witchcraft was heresy, orders the
Inquisition at Carcassonne to seize
the property of Witches, sorcerers, and
those who make wax images, 1320

23 Thursday
1st ♎
☽ enters ♏ 4:50 am
♇ D 11:06 am
Color: Violet

*When seeking a fair decision, burn a brown
candle while asking for justice to prevail*

24 Friday
1st ♏
Color: Green

Set in Eastern Standard Time (EST)

Salsa

3 medium tomatoes, finely diced
½ medium onion, finely diced
½ green pepper, finely diced
2 tbs. cilantro, finely chopped
1 jalapeño pepper, finely chopped
1 clove garlic, finely chopped
½ tsp. cumin
½ tsp. oregano
⅛ tsp. salt
1 tbs. lemon juice
1 tbs. lime juice
½ tsp. grated lemon zest (the yellow part of the peel)

Mix all ingredients and refrigerate at least two hours. If you like a chunky sauce, chop vegetables by hand—a blender or food processor may turn tomatoes and green peppers into mush. If you like a really hot salsa, use 2 jalapeños. This recipe is perfect for when that fertility spell works a little too well on your tomatoes, and you need to find new ways to eat them!

—Magenta Griffith

☾ Saturday
1st ♏
☽ v/c 6:16 am
☽ enters ♐ 9:59 am
2nd Quarter 2:55 pm
Color: Indigo

26 Sunday
2nd ♐
⚷ D 4:19 am
♀ enters ♌ 11:12 pm
Color: Gold

To relieve stress, flood your altar
space with flames of blue candles,
and dine on blue-colored foods

August/September

27 Monday

2nd ♐
☽ v/c 7:50 am
☽ enters ♑ 7:02 pm
Color: Silver

There came into my hands the reports of certain matters, from which I learned, as I had not hitherto done, that Witches were wont to fly off from their marriage beds to their assemblies.
—Nicholas Rémy, *Daemonolatria*

28 Tuesday

2nd ♑
Color: Red

29 Wednesday

2nd ♑
Color: Peach

They found a pipe of ointment, wherewith she greased a staffe, upon which she ambled and galloped through thicke and thin.
—R. Holinshed, chronicler, from the Alice Kyteler Witch trial

30 Thursday

2nd ♑
☽ v/c 1:28 am
☽ enters ♒ 6:47 am
Color: Green

If your new home has a rowan tree on the property, all who dwell therein will be blessed; in gratitude, chant Druidic rites

31 Friday

2nd ♒
☿ enters ♎ 7:37 pm
Color: Rose

Birthday of Raymond Buckland, who, along with his wife Rosemary, is generally credited with bringing Gardnerian Wicca to the United States

Harvest Moon

Offerings demonstrate prosperity and bounty among many different Native American tribes. This Harvest Moon ritual is a way of saying thank you to the Creator, Earth Mother, the community, and special people:

First, hang dried ears of corn and place bowls of colorful squash around your home to show your appreciation of the harvest season. Now, gather different vegetables, herbs, fruits, nuts, and other foods into a large basket. Take the basket, a pen, a piece of paper, a lighter, and incense prepared from a mixture of dried cedar, sage, copal, bearberry, and red willow herbs, and go outdoors. Dig a hole in the earth, and place the basket within. Light the incense. Face north to form a thanksgiving circle around the basket, offering thanks as you face each direction—home, resources, health (north); wisdom (east); accomplishments (south); relationships (west). Write your prayers for the next harvest year on the paper and place them in the basket. Cover the basket with soil, giving all to Mother Earth with prayers of thanksgiving. Repeat your prayers every time you store away food for the coming winter.

—Marguerite Elsbeth

---

1 Saturday
2nd ≈
☽ v/c 12:36 pm
☽ enters ♓ 7:32 pm
Color: Brown

☺ Sunday
2nd ♓
Full Moon 4:43 pm
Color: Gold

Celtic Tree Month of Vine begins
Harvest Moon
Birthday of Reverend Paul
Beyerl, Wiccan author

September

3 Monday
3rd ♓
Color: Lavender

Labor Day

4 Tuesday
3rd ♓
☽ v/c 3:37 am
☽ enters ♈ 7:58 am
Color: White

Witches can control not only rain
and hail and wind but even
lightning, with God's permission.
—Francesco Guazzo,
Compendium Maleficarum

5 Wednesday
3rd ♈
Color: Yellow

Come hither, sir, come hither, my lord,
let down your locks so long and flowing.
—Malay invocation of the wind

6 Thursday
3rd ♈
☽ v/c 5:31 pm
☽ enters ♉ 7:18 pm
Color: White

7 Friday
3rd ♉
Color: Pink

Use honeycomb as an altar decoration
when invoking Venus, since bees and
bliss connote the venerated goddess

September

I am the Harvester, the Reaper of Grain
And all that has ripened is in my domain
Herbs and flowers and honey are mine
And nuts and grain and fruit on the vine
I pick and I pluck, taking only the best
I strip the fields so that they can rest
I shake the trees and they are bare, too
But I cannot rest; I've still much to do
The lessons of Karma completed and won
Must be reaped, too, before I am done
And as I gather, each spirit is blessed
And furthered along in Cosmic success
                                        —Dorothy Morrison

---

8 Saturday
3rd ♉
♂ enters ♑ 12:51 pm
☽ v/c 1:30 pm
Color: Blue

Founding of the Theosophical
Society by H. P. Blavatsky, Henry
Steele Olcott, and others, 1875

---

9 Sunday
3rd ♉
☽ enters ♊ 4:41 am
Color: Orange

◯ **Monday**
3rd ♊
4th Quarter 1:59 pm
☽ v/c 8:42 pm
Color: Gray

Birthday of Carl Llewellyn
Weschcke, owner and president
of Llewellyn Publications

11 Tuesday
4th ♊
☽ enters ♋ 11:09 am
Color: Red

Birthday of Silver RavenWolf,
Wiccan author
Birthday of the Wiccan Pagan
Press Alliance (WPPA)

12 Wednesday
4th ♋
☽ v/c 10:16 pm
Color: White

And to Solomon we taught the
use of blowing winds that
moved with his command.
—*Al Koran*

13 Thursday
4th ♋
☽ enters ♌ 2:16 pm
Color: Green

14 Friday
4th ♌
Color: White

Phillip IV of France draws up
the order for the arrest of
the French Templars, 1306
Birthday of Henry Cornelius Agrippa,
scholar and magician, 1486

15 Saturday

4th ♌
☽ v/c 3:35 am
☽ enters ♍ 2:39 pm
Color: Gray

16 Sunday

4th ♍
Color: Yellow

To magnify the powers of a particular candle
during ritual work, also light a white candle
and allow the two to burn in unison

☽ Monday
4th ♍
New Moon 5:27 am
☽ v/c 5:27 am
☽ enters ♎ 2:00 pm
Color: White

Bewitched debuts on ABC-TV, 1964

18 Tuesday
1st ♎
Color: Gray

Rosh Hashanah

19 Wednesday
1st ♎
☽ v/c 11:38 am
☽ enters ♏ 2:27 pm
Color: Brown

Congressman Robert S. Walker introduces HR-3389 to amend IRS rules to read, "any religious or apostolic organization which has as its primary purpose the promotion of Witchcraft or which has a substantial interest in the promotion of witchcraft shall not be exempt from taxation," 1985

20 Thursday
1st ♏
♀ enters ♍ 9:09 pm
Color: Turquoise

When conducting a protection spell, light a black candle to absorb negative energy

21 Friday
1st ♏
☽ v/c 4:09 pm
☽ enters ♐ 6:02 pm
Color: Peach

Mabon

Mabon celebrates the harvesting of the fruits and berries that will sustain us through the dark winter days to come. For this ritual you will need five glasses of berry wine and a place outside where these can be emptied onto the ground. This is best done at dusk or dawn when light and dark seem to be held in perfect balance, just as they will be throughout the twenty-four hour equinox period. In a circle around you, place one glass at each of the cardinal

points: north (earth), east (air), south (fire), and west (water). Place the other in the center. Starting at any point in the circle, begin moving counterclockwise, pouring the wine onto the ground to pay homage to the nature spirits or elementals who stand guard over the land as it prepares for its winter nap. Lastly, empty the wine in the center as an offering and libation to the Goddess, who is resting after giving birth to the harvest.

—Edain McCoy

22 Saturday

1st ♐
☉ enters ♎ 6:04 pm
Color: Indigo

Mabon/Fall Equinox
Sun enters Libra

23 Sunday

1st ♐
☽ v/c 7:32 pm
Color: Peach

If I command the Moon, it will come down; and if I wish to withhold the day, night will linger over my head; and again, if I wish to embark on the sea, I need no ship; and if I wish to fly through the air, I am freed from my weight.
—Greek magical papyrus

◐ Monday

1st ♐
☽ enters ♑ 1:48 am
2nd Quarter 4:31 am
Color: Silver

*To shield magical elixirs in your
pantry from harm or spoilage,
store with freshly ground peppercorns*

25 Tuesday

2nd ♑
Color: Black

Senate passes an amendment (705)
attached by Senator Jesse Helms to House
Resolution 3036 (1986 budget bill) on
fiscal funding for agencies, denying tax
exempt status to any organization that
espouses satanism or Witchcraft, 1985

26 Wednesday

2nd ♑
☽ v/c 9:38 am
☽ enters ♒ 1:05 pm
♄ ℞ 7:04 pm
Color: Yellow

Leo Martello is initiated
into a Sicilian coven
Joan Wiliford hanged at Faversham,
England, 1645; she testified that
the Devil came to her in the form of a
black dog that she called "Bunnie"

27 Thursday

2nd ♒
Color: Violet

Yom Kippur

28 Friday

2nd ♒
Color: Rose

Set in Eastern Standard Time (EST)

Stuffed Grape Leaves

10 grape leaves
½ cup rice
½ cup chickpeas
1 onion, minced
2 cloves garlic
1 tbs. parsley
Salt
Pepper

Blanch the grape leaves in boiling water for about five minutes. Combine the rice with the chickpeas (either canned or cooked), the minced onion, garlic, parsley, and seasoning. Place a tablespoon of this mixture on each leaf, roll up in a cylinder and press together with your hand. Cook them for about 30 minutes with enough water to cover (if you wish, you can substitute tomato juice seasoned with lemon for water). They may be eaten hot or cold. If you have no grape leaves, cabbage leaves (remove the spine) or even lettuce leaves may be used. If you are pressed for time, layer the ingredients in a casserole dish and bake until warm through.

—Breid Foxsong

---

29 Saturday
2nd ≈
☽ v/c 12:27 am
☽ enters ♓ 1:50 am
Color: Brown

*Use orange peel in cooking
to strengthen mental capacities*

---

30 Sunday
2nd ♓
☽ v/c 8:02 am
Color: Gold

Celtic Tree Month of Ivy begins

October

1 Monday

2nd ♓
☽ enters ♈ 2:08 pm
☿ ℞ 2:24 pm
Color: Gray

Birthday of Isaac Bonewitz,
Druid, magician, and Witch

Birthday of Annie Besant,
Theosophical Society President

☺ Tuesday

2nd ♈
Full Moon 8:49 am
Color: Red

Sukkot begins
Blood Moon
Birthday of Timothy Roderick,
Wiccan author

3 Wednesday

3rd ♈
☽ v/c 11:44 pm
Color: Yellow

4 Thursday

3rd ♈
☽ enters ♉ 1:01 am
Color: Turquoise

President Reagan signs JR 165 making
1983 "The Year of the Bible" (public law
#9728Q); the law states that the Bible is
the word of God and urges a return to
"traditional" Christian values, 1982

5 Friday

3rd ♉
☽ v/c 5:33 pm
Color: White

If you feel no zeal in your life,
integrate ambergris oil into a rite
intended to awaken love and emotion

Blood Moon

Your ancestors—deceased cousins, aunts, uncles, sisters, brothers, mothers, fathers, and grandparents—are the ghosts of your collective past. The Blood Moon is a time to honor them with this ritual feast:

Plan a menu of traditional family dishes. Be sure to include a bottle of red wine (or an alcohol-free grape beverage). Set the table using a black tablecloth and orange napkins, your best dinnerware and glasses. Place two tapered candles colored black and orange, a vase of white lilies, a bell, and photographs of your ancestors in the center. When all is ready, light the candles, sit down, and silently recall your ancestors. Stand, pour the wine, ring the bell three times, and share the following toast: "Merry meet, (name your ancestors here)!" Raise your wine glass and say: "We are the blood of your blood. May our earthly lives fulfill your otherworld dreams with goodness. Come, share this feast." Eat and drink in their honor, sharing your fondest memories about each one. When you are finished, ring the bell three times and say: "All my relations, blessed be."

—Marguerite Elsbeth

---

6 Saturday

3rd ☉
☽ enters ♊ 10:12 am
Color: Gray

---

7 Sunday

3rd ♊
Color: Yellow

Birthday of Arnold Crowther, stage
magician and Gardnerian Witch, 1909

October

8 Monday

3rd ♊
☽ v/c 11:23 am
☽ enters ♋ 5:19 pm
Color: Lavender

Sukkot ends
Columbus Day (observed)

○ Tuesday

3rd ♋
4th Quarter 11:20 pm
Color: White

*Drink coconut milk as a
protection potion in ritual work*

10 Wednesday

4th ♋
☽ v/c 12:47 pm
☽ enters ♌ 9:54 pm
Color: Peach

Then she stood up; and pronouncing
some words to me unintelligible, she said,
"By virtue of my necromancy, become
thou half stone and half man,"
and the citizens she transformed
by her enchantments into fishes.
—*Arabian Nights*

11 Thursday

4th ♌
Color: White

12 Friday

4th ♌
☽ v/c 11:34 am
☽ enters ♍ 11:58 pm
Color: Pink

Birthday of Aleister Crowley

Jacques de Molay, head of the French
Templars and godfather to Phillip IV's
son, is honored as a pallbearer at the
funeral of the king's sister-in-law, 1306;
the next day Phillip has all of the
Templars seized, including de Molay

13 Saturday
4th ♍
Color: Indigo

Jacques de Molay and other
French Templars arrested by
order of King Phillip IV, 1306

14 Sunday
4th ♍
☽ v/c 11:52 pm
Color: Orange

October

15 Monday

4th ♍
☽ enters ♎ 12:26 am
♀ enters ♎ 6:42 am
Color: White

*Touch the earth, spit downward,
and chant twenty-seven times,
fasting: O Earth, keep the pain, and
health with me remain in my feet.
—Charm to cure gout
from Roman author Varro*

☽ Tuesday

4th ♎
New Moon 2:23 pm
☽ v/c 2:23 pm
Color: Gray

*To gain magical insight, integrate
mushrooms into your cooking repertoire*

17 Wednesday

1st ♎
☽ enters ♏ 1:03 am
Ψ D 8:48 pm
Color: Brown

18 Thursday

1st ♏
☽ v/c 5:30 pm
Color: Violet

19 Friday

1st ♏
☽ enters ♐ 3:47 am
Color: Rose

*Since seashells are a consummate
symbol of the Goddess, serve charged
seashell pasta at a ritual gathering*

October

I sing of Wisdom, of future and change
I am familiar, but hauntingly strange
I live in challenge and obstacles turned
I am experience and lessons hard-earned
I come from examining every conclusion
(And balances added without delusion)
From knowing within and acting without
Questions and answers, reason and doubt
I am all strands in the Great Cosmic Web
The Conscious Collective that cannot ebb
I'm all who have lived and all yet to be
These form my steps—come dance with me
—Dorothy Morrison

20 Saturday
1st ♐
Color: Blue

Birthday of Selena Fox, Circle Sanctuary

21 Sunday
1st ♐
☽ v/c 6:42 am
☽ enters ♑ 10:11 am
Color: Gold

22 Monday

1st ♑
☿ D 7:24 pm
Color: Silver

Now with magic howlings she keeps
the swarms of the grave before her:
now she sprinkles them with
milk and bids them retreat.
—Tibellus

◐ Tuesday

1st ♑
☉ enters ♏ 3:26 am
☽ v/c 3:11 pm
☽ enters ♒ 8:26 pm
2nd Quarter 9:58 pm
Color: Black

Sun enters Scorpio

24 Wednesday

2nd ♒
Color: White

Hearken to my prayer; Free me
from bewitchment; Loosen my sin;
Let there be turned aside whatever
evil may come to cut off my life.
—Babylonian incantation from the
Tablet of Assurbanipal

25 Thursday

2nd ♒
☽ v/c 2:32 pm
Color: Turquoise

Jacques de Molay first interrogated
after Templar arrest, 1306

26 Friday

2nd ♒
☽ enters ♓ 8:56 am
Color: Peach

Sibyl Leek dies of cancer, 1982
De Molay and thirty-one other
Templars confess to heresy in front
of an assembly of clergy; all later
recant their confessions, 1306

Harvest Treats

6 oz. cream cheese
1 cup butter
2 cups flour
2 cups light brown sugar
2 eggs
2 tsp. vanilla
4 tbs. melted butter
¼ tsp. salt
1½ cups walnuts or pecans, chopped

To make dough, combine cream cheese, butter, and flour. Let sit at room temperature for about an hour. For filling, combine brown sugar, eggs, vanilla, melted butter, and salt in a large bowl. Form dough into little walnut-sized balls. Using mini-muffin pans, line each cup with the dough by pressing along sides and bottom. Fill bottom of each cup with nuts, then add about 2 tsp. of the filling. Cups should be half full to prevent running over while baking. Bake at 350° for 25 minutes. Cool and remove from pan. Makes about 7 dozen treats.

—Kirin Lee

27 Saturday
2nd ♓
♂ enters ♒ 12:19 pm
☽ v/c 4:31 pm
Color: Brown

Circle Sanctuary founded, 1974

28 Sunday
2nd ♓
☽ enters ♈ 9:15 pm
Color: Peach

Daylight Saving Time ends at 2:00 am
Celtic Tree Month of Reed begins

October/November

29 Monday

2nd ♈
Color: Gray

MacGregor Mathers issues manifesto calling himself supreme leader of the Golden Dawn; all members had to sign an oath of fealty to him, 1896

Birthday of Frater Zarathustra, who founded the Temple of Truth in 1972

30 Tuesday

2nd ♈
☽ v/c 2:17 pm
♅ D 5:55 pm
Color: Red

House-Senate conferees drop the Jesse Helms-sponsored Senate provision barring the IRS from granting tax-exempt status to groups that promote satanism or Witchcraft, stating that the provision came under the jurisdiction of the House Ways and Means Committee, 1985

31 Wednesday

2nd ♈
☽ enters ♉ 7:48 am
Color: Yellow

Samhain/Halloween

Charter date for Covenant of the Goddess

New Reformed Orthodox Order of the Golden Dawn formed, 1967

Martin Luther pins his 95 theses to the door of Wittenburg Castle Church, igniting the Protestant revolution, 1517

☺ Thursday

2nd ♉
Full Moon 12:41 am
☽ v/c 11:20 pm
Color: Turquoise

All Saints' Day

Mourning Moon

Aquarian Tabernacle Church established in the United States, 1979

2 Friday

3rd ♉
♃ Rx 10:35 am
☽ enters ♊ 4:12 pm
Color: White

Circle Sanctuary purchases land for nature preserve, 1983

Samhain/Halloween

In many traditions, Samhain marks the spiritual New Year, a time when we want to focus on our connection to the past and to the future. To ancient peoples, stones represented the link between ourselves and those who walked our Earth before us and would do so after us. This is still seen today in the New Year's rituals of South Pacific islanders and in Jewish cemeteries the world over. To honor those who came before, gather some interesting stones—

large, but small enough to carry comfortably—and take them to any place that makes you feel connected to your ancestors. Graveyards, a home, or a piece of land are all appropriate. Speak out loud your desire to connect with those who once walked in this place and invite them to link more closely with you. Place the stones firmly into the ground, knowing that they will be there always, connecting you to the entirety of your family tree from oldest root to newest bud.

—Edain McCoy

---

3 Saturday
3rd ♊
Color: Brown

Petronella de Meath, servant of Lady Alice Kyteler, is executed in the first recorded Witch burning in Ireland, 1324; the Kyteler trial is significant because Lady Kyteler was one of the first Witches said to be the head of an *organized* heretical group; previously the Church believed that Witch groups had no formal structure

---

4 Sunday
3rd ♊
☽ v/c 2:45 pm
☽ enters ♋ 10:44 pm
Color: Peach

---

5 Monday
3rd ♋
Color: Lavender

Catholic Guy Fawkes tries to blow up the Protestant-sympathetic House of Lords, 1605; Fawkes is executed, and Parliament makes this a day of thanksgiving; Guy Fawkes' Day took the place of All Hallows Eve and All Saints' Day for many Protestant English who did not celebrate saints' days, and in some areas the holidays merged

6 Tuesday
3rd ♋
Color: White

General Election Day
Samhain cross-quarter day
(Sun reaches 15° Scorpio)

7 Wednesday
3rd ♋
☽ v/c 2:10 am
☽ enters ♌ 3:34 am
☿ enters ♏ 2:53 pm
Color: Peach

☾ Thursday
3rd ♌
4th Quarter 7:21 am
♀ enters ♏ 8:28 am
☽ v/c 3:30 pm
Color: White

Marriage of Patricia and Arnold Crowther officiated by Gerald Gardner, 1960
Sentencing of Witches in Basque Zugarramurdi trial, 1610

9 Friday
4th ♌
☽ enters ♍ 6:49 am
Color: Pink

Patricia and Arnold Crowther married in civil ceremony, 1960
Gwyddion Pendderwen dies in car accident

Mourning Moon

Descansos are crosses that traditionally mark a person's initial or final resting place, such as a gravesite or the location of a fatality. They may also serve as symbolic reminders for the little deaths and losses you experience every day. These Mourning Moon rituals will help you to honor the dead, release your sad memories, and put your grief to rest:

Make a small descanso for each of your losses using sticks or twigs. Paint them white and decorate. Release the person, place, or thing symbolized by each descanso as you go. Place them in a memory box, or burn them when you are through.

Light a white candle and burn your favorite incense. Fashion a cross out of materials representing your memories and experiences. Then add something for each loss you have suffered—photographs, jewelry, flowers, ribbons, fabric, or feathers. Display the cross on your altar or hang it on the wall. Continue to add something every time you know failure, a setback, or feel that a portion of yourself has died.

—Marguerite Elsbeth

10 Saturday
4th ♍
☽ v/c 1:40 pm
Color: Gray

When summoning the fey folk, proffer stuffed mushroom caps in a gesture of hospitality

11 Sunday
4th ♍
☽ enters ♎ 8:53 am
Color: Orange

Veterans Day

November

12 Monday
4th ♎
☽ v/c 7:42 pm
Color: White

*Millions of spiritual creatures walk
the earth unseen, both when we
wake and when we sleep.*
—John Milton

13 Tuesday
4th ♎
☽ enters ♏ 10:44 am
Color: Gray

*Eggs draw negativity from the body;
be sure to always salt an egg prior to eating:
this will increase extraction of impure forces*

14 Wednesday
4th ♏
Color: Brown

☽ Thursday
4th ♏
New Moon 1:40 am
☽ v/c 1:40 am
☽ enters ♐ 1:51 pm
Color: Violet

Aquarian Tabernacle Church
established in Canada, 1993
Death of Albertus Magnus, a
ceremonial magician who allegedly
discovered the philosopher's stone

16 Friday
1st ♐
Color: Rose

17 Saturday
1st ♐
☽ v/c 3:14 am
☽ enters ♑ 7:40 pm
Color: Indigo

Ramadan begins
Birthday of Israel Regardie, occultist
and member of the OTO, 1907

18 Sunday
1st ♑
Color: Gold

Aleister Crowley initiated into the Golden
Dawn as Frater Perdurabo, 1898

November

19 Monday

1st ♑

Color: Silver

Birthday of Theodore
Parker Mills, Wiccan elder

20 Tuesday

1st ♑

☽ v/c 12:57 am

☽ enters ♒ 4:55 am

Color: Black

Church of All Worlds
incorporates in Australia, 1992

21 Wednesday

1st ♒

Color: White

○ Thursday

1st ♒

☉ enters ♐ 1:00 am

☽ v/c 2:37 am

☽ enters ♓ 4:52 pm

2nd Quarter 6:21 pm

Color: Turquoise

Thanksgiving Day

Sun enters Sagittarius

Phillip IV pressures Pope Clement to issue
bull *Pastoralis Praeminentiae* calling for
monarchs of Western Europe to arrest
any Templars in their territories, 1306;
Clement agrees after a high-level Templar
confesses he denied Christ at his reception

23 Friday

2nd ♓

Color: Peach

Birthday of Lady Tamara Von Forslun,
founder of the Church of Wicca and the
Aquarian Tabernacle Church in Australia

Frustration Tea

2 tea bags of English Breakfast,
   opened and emptied (may substitute
   2 tsp. of loose tea)
1 tsp. chamomile, dried
1 tsp. hyssop, dried
1 tsp. raspberry leaf, dried and crushed

This tea is fruity and smooth, with a reddish tint. You can make this tea in an automatic tea maker, or use two pots, straining the herbs from one to another using boiling water. Add sugar and milk (not cream) to taste. If stress is leading to headaches, add a teaspoon of wood betony, rosemary, or skullcap to the tea. Enjoy your soothing drink, and you'll be ready to face the chaotic energies of life with a smile.

—Ann Moura

24 Saturday
2nd ♓
Color: Blue

Burdock is an invaluable shielding
ingredient for protection amulets and sachets

25 Sunday
2nd ♓
☽ v/c 12:29 am
☽ enters ♈ 5:21 am
Color: Peach

Celtic Tree Month of Elder begins
Dr. John Dee notes Edward
Kelly's death in his diary, 1595

November/December

26 Monday
2nd ♈
☿ enters ♐ 1:23 pm
☽ v/c 11:43 pm
Color: Gray

> Witchcraft is so enduring that it admits
> of no remedy by human operation.
> —St. Thomas Aquinas

27 Tuesday
2nd ♈
☽ enters ♉ 4:06 pm
Color: Red

28 Wednesday
2nd ♉
Color: Yellow

> To assert that acts of Witchcraft are
> impossible is an erroneous belief.
> —Kramer and Sprenger,
> *Malleus Maleficarum*

29 Thursday
2nd ♉
☽ v/c 6:21 pm
Color: Turquoise

> *An infusion of boneset dispersed in a home
> will keep evil elements from gaining entry*

☺ Friday
2nd ♉
☽ enters ♊ 12:04 am
Full Moon 3:49 pm
Color: White

Blue Moon

Birthday of Oberon Zell,
Church of All Worlds

Henge of Keltria incorporates as
a nonprofit organization, 1995

Father Urbain Grandier imprisoned in
France for bewitching nuns, 1633

December

I am the starlight that twinkles on high
Sparkling like diamonds on the ebony sky
Mariner's friend and astronomer's quest
Our Mother's glorious blanket and guest
But I am, too, something deeper and more
(Almost forgotten, but written in lore)
So I call out to you and beckon you near
Enticing you as from the window you peer
Bring me your wishes and honest desires—
Passionate fancies and unquiet fires—
Give them to me with a fervent petition
And I'll ignite each into total fruition

       —Dorothy Morrison

---

1 Saturday
3rd ♊
☽ v/c 8:48 pm
Color: Brown

Birthday of Anodea Judith,
President, Church of All Worlds

---

2 Sunday
3rd ♊
☽ enters ♋ 5:30 am
♀ enters ♐ 6:11 am
Color: Yellow

December

3 Monday
3rd ♋
☽ v/c 6:04 am
Color: Gray

*Offer strawberries and cream to the
Bean-Tighe faery know as the Woman of the
House; she'll watch over the children and pets*

4 Tuesday
3rd ♋
☽ enters ♌ 9:15 am
Color: Red

5 Wednesday
3rd ♌
Color: White

Death of Aleister Crowley, 1947

Pope Innocent VIII reverses the
Canon Episcopi by issuing the bull
Summis Desiderantes Affectibus, removing
obstacles to inquisitors, 1484

6 Thursday
3rd ♌
☽ v/c 9:20 am
☽ enters ♍ 12:11 pm
Color: Violet

Birthday of Dion Fortune, member
of the Golden Dawn, 1890

Death of Jacob Sprenger, coauthor
of the *Malleus Maleficarum*, 1495

☽ Friday
3rd ♍
4th Quarter 2:52 pm
☽ v/c 5:57 pm
Color: White

8 Saturday

4th ♍
☽ enters ♎ 2:57 pm
♂ enters ♓ 4:52 pm
Color: Blue

Mercury, inventor of incantations,
was wont to be invoked in the rites of
magicians, and Venus, who entices
the mind, and the Moon, aware of
night's mystery, and Hecate, mistress
of the spirits of the dead.
—Apuleius

9 Sunday

4th ♎
Color: Gold

December

10 Monday
4th ♎
☽ v/c 3:43 am
☽ enters ♏ 6:09 pm
Color: White

Hanukkah begins

11 Tuesday
4th ♏
⚷ enters ♑ 6:04 pm
Color: Blue

Have you heard that magic is an art
acceptable to the immortal gods; a
notable art since the age of Zoroaster
and Oromazus, the inventors, and
handmaiden to the heavenly beings?
—Apuleius

12 Wednesday
4th ♏
☽ v/c 7:48 am
☽ enters ♐ 10:30 pm
Color: Peach

13 Thursday
4th ♐
Color: Green

*When calling upon the four corners, use
sandalwood for altar blessings; it composes
the senses and sets the tone for reflection*

☽ Friday
4th ♐
New Moon 3:47 pm
Color: Pink

Solar eclipse 3:53 pm, 22° ♐ 56'

Set in Eastern Standard Time (EST)

Reindeer Sandwiches

1 slice bread for each sandwich
Pretzels
Marshmallows or maraschino cherries
Raisins
Peanut butter

Spread the bread liberally with peanut butter, then use a sharp knife to cut it diagonally in two. Place a large pretzel in each corner of the diagonal cut to form antlers, two raisins in the center of the triangle for eyes, and a marshmallow or cherry on the lower point for the nose.

—Dorothy Morrison

15 Saturday

1st ♐
☽ v/c 3:24 am
☽ enters ♑ 4:48 am
☿ enters ♑ 2:55 pm
Color: Gray

Ramadan ends

16 Sunday

1st ♑
☽ v/c 4:35 am
Color: Orange

When spellcasting for riches, make
an offer to Copia, goddess of plenty;
blackberry leaves garnishing the altar
will add to the potency of the spell

December

17 Monday
1st ♑
☽ enters ♒ 1:43 pm
Color: Silver

Hanukkah ends

18 Tuesday
1st ♒
Color: Gray

*Frivolous and false, it (magic) still
contains some element of truth in it.
—Pliny the Elder*

19 Wednesday
1st ♒
☽ v/c 9:41 pm
Color: Yellow

20 Thursday
1st ♒
☽ enters ♓ 1:09 am
Color: White

*Decorate the door to your home
with a wreath of bay laurel
for a traditional Yule embellishment*

21 Friday
1st ♓
☉ enters ♑ 2:21 pm
Color: Rose

Yule/Winter Solstice
Sun enters Capricorn

Set in Eastern Standard Time (EST)

Yule

Yule marks the beginning of a new solar year. Honor the newly born Sun God by festively decorating your home, lavishing everything with light, and staying up late into the night playing "midwife" to the Sun's mother, our Goddess. As with any form of creation, birth is not a quick process, so plan to make this ritual last over the next thirty-six hours or so. In frequent meditation, project loving energy to her as she struggles to give birth. As
the dawn approaches, welcome the newborn God of the waxing year with acorns, the symbol of the oak tree, which is representative of his next half-year's reign. Make a breakfast featuring other nut products: breads, cakes, and butters are all easy to find or make. The following evening, offer a prayer of thanks to your deities as Yule Day closes and you note that the Sun has set just a bit later in the evening than the night before.

—Edain McCoy

○ Saturday

1st ♓
☽ v/c 3:44 am
☽ enters ♈ 1:45 pm
2nd Quarter 3:56 pm
Color: Indigo

Janet and Stewart Farrar begin
their first coven together, 1970

---

23 Sunday

2nd ♈
Color: Yellow

December

24 Monday
2nd ♈
☽ v/c 10:21 pm
Color: White

Christmas Eve
Celtic Tree Month of Birch begins

25 Tuesday
2nd ♈
☽ enters ♉ 1:12 am
Color: Gray

Christmas Day
Feast of Frau Holle, Germanic
weather goddess who was believed
to travel through the world to
watch people's deeds; she blessed
the good and punished the bad

26 Wednesday
2nd ♉
♀ enters ♑ 2:25 am
☽ v/c 7:22 pm
Color: Brown

Kwanzaa begins
Dr. Fian arraigned for twenty counts
of Witchcraft and treason

27 Thursday
2nd ♉
☽ enters ♊ 9:39 am
Color: Rose

Birthday of Gerina Dunwich,
Wiccan Author

28 Friday
2nd ♊
Color: Peach

Long Nights Moon

December is a time of renewal and rebirth. Celebrate the Sun's return by decorating your home with evergreen boughs, a Yule log, and a small evergreen tree. You may want to include a wreath to represent the wheel of the year. Make mead, cook up some Yuletide goodies, play Celtic music, and invite friends to participate in this Long Nights Moon ritual:

Set up an altar in the corner of your living room. Cover the altar with a green cloth and place upon it a variety of fresh evergreens along with two candles, red and green. Assemble your guests, and cast a magic circle around the altar. Light the candles. Now, pull the red candle toward you, prompting all to say: "The Sun passes, the Sun returns." Blow out the candle, relight it, and move it back. Now pull the green candle forward, as all say: "Greenery passes, greenery returns." Blow out the green candle, relight it, and move it back in place.

Now carry on with any seasonal activities that you had planned for the evening—exchanging gifts, singing carols, or decorating the tree.

—Marguerite Elsbeth

---

29 Saturday
2nd ♊
☽ v/c 1:24 am
☽ enters ♋ 2:40 pm
Color: Brown

According to ancient lore, if you
eat sage daily you will live a long life

☺ Sunday
2nd ♋
Full Moon 5:40 am
Color: Gold

Long Nights Moon
Lunar eclipse 5:30 am, 8° ♋ 48'

December

31 Monday
3rd ♋
☽ v/c 8:43 am
☽ enters ♌ 5:09 pm
Color: Lavender

New Year's Eve
Castle of Countess Bathory of
Hungary raided, 1610; accused of
practicing black magic, she murdered
scores of the local townsfolk; she
was walled up in a room in
her castle, where she later died

1 Tuesday
3rd ♌
Color: Peach

New Year's Day
Kwanzaa ends

2 Wednesday
3rd ♌
☽ v/c 6:13 pm
☽ enters ♍ 6:34 pm
Color: Purple

3 Thursday
3rd ♍
☿ enters ♒ 4:38 pm
Color: Green

4 Friday
3rd ♍
☽ v/c 2:30 am
☽ enters ♎ 8:23 pm
Color: White

Set in Eastern Standard Time (EST)

December

I am the Moon. I shine through the night
In radiant, splendorous, silvery light
I rule the gardens and I rule the tides
I rule emotions and thoughts held inside
Mine is the World of Spirit, and deep
Within all My glory its secrets I keep
But I give direction and I lead the way
Exposing it all while sleeping, you lay
For as you rest, My teaching begins
Consistent and constant without any end
So nod off to sleep; rest long and well
As I weave the threads of My magic spell

—Dorothy Morrison

◗ Saturday
3rd ♎
4th Quarter 10:55 pm
Color: Red

6 Sunday
4th ♎
☽ v/c 11:05 am
☽ enters ♏ 11:41 pm
Color: Pink

Twelfth Night/Epiphany

About the Authors

ESTELLE DANIELS is a professional astrologer and high priestess of Eclectic Wicca. She is the author of *Astrologickal Magic*, a guide to using astrology and magic, and coauthor of *Pocket Guide to Wicca*. Estelle has a private astrological practice and travels to festivals, bookstores, and conferences in the United States, lecturing and teaching.

GERINA DUNWICH is a high priestess of the Old Religion, a professional astrologer, and the author of numerous books on Wicca and spellcasting. A lifelong student of the occult arts and metaphysical sciences, Gerina is the founder of the Pagan Poets Society, the Wheel of Wisdom School, Golden Isis Press, and the Bast-Wicca tradition.

MARGUERITE ELSBETH (Raven Hawk) is a professional diviner and a student of Native American and European folk healing. She is coauthor of *The Silver Wheel: Women's Myths and Mysteries in the Celtic Tradition* with Kenneth Johnson, and author of *Crystal Medicine: Working with Crystals, Gems, and Minerals*.

BREID FOXSONG is a British Traditional Wiccan who has been practicing for more than twenty years. She is the former editor of *Sacred Hart* magazine and has had articles published in other magazines, ranging from *Green Egg* to *Craft/Crafts*.

YASMINE GALENORN has practiced the Craft since 1980. She teaches classes on natural magic, leads public and private rituals, and is a professional tarot reader with a loyal clientele. She is the author of *Embracing the Moon*, *Trancing the Witch's Wheel*, and *Dancing with the Sun*.

MAGENTA GRIFFITH has been a Witch for over twenty-five years, a High Priestess for over twelve years, and is a founding member of the coven Prodea, which has been practicing for nearly twenty years. She presents workshops and classes at festivals and gatherings around the Midwest.

LADY GYNGERE OF THE GROVE wrote the herbal sayings scattered throughout the datebook. A journalist and cookbook editor, Lady Gyngere is an internationally recognized authority on specialty food and beverages. She is the culinary delights columnist for *Renaissance Magazine*. Her expertise includes medieval kitchens and equipment, great hall feasting, courtly love, ale as a cultural artifact, and dining etiquette.

KIRIN LEE writes and does graphic design for a science fiction magazine and is managing editor of a rock music magazine. When she is not writing articles, she is writing science fiction, and is currently working on a *Star Trek* novel and beginning a Pagan parenting handbook.

EDAIN MCCOY has been a Witch since 1981, and today is a part of the Wittan Irish Pagan Tradition and a Priestess of Brighid and elder within that tradition. Edain is the author of *Witta: An Irish Pagan Tradition; A Witch's Guide to Faery Folk; The Sabbats; Mountain Magic; Entering the Summerland; Inside A Witches' Coven;* and *Celtic Women's Spirituality.*

DOROTHY MORRISON is a Third Degree High Priestess of the Georgian Tradition, and has spent many years teaching the Craft to students across the United States and in Australia. She is the author of *Magical Needlework, Everyday Magic, In Praise of the Crone,* the forthcoming *Bud, Blossom & Leaf: A Magical Herb Gardener's Handbook,* and *The Whimsical Tarot.*

ANN MOURA (Aoumiel) was raised in a family tradition of three generations and has practiced as a solitary Witch for over thirty-five years. She is the author of the Llewellyn books *Dancing Shadows, Green Witchcraft,* and *Green Witchcraft II: Working with Light and Shadow.*

JAMI SHOEMAKER has been practicing Witchcraft for eighteen years, and was initiated as a priestess in the Rowan Tree Church in 1992. She has taught a variety of Craft-related subjects, and has worked to help educate the general public about her religion. She has a degree in vocal music, a background in theatre and dance, and has always enjoyed writing.

STEVEN POSCH is the founding member of Prodea and of the Covenant of the Goddess' Northern Dawn Council. His writings have appeared in many publications, including: *Green Egg, Mezlim, Circle Network News, The Witchtower,* and *The James White Review.* He is coauthor of several books and has a folktale collection coming out in 2001.

Name:

Address, City, State, Zip:

Home Phone: Office Phone:

E-mail: Birthday:

Name:

Address, City, State, Zip:

Home Phone: Office Phone:

E-mail: Birthday:

Name:

Address, City, State, Zip:

Home Phone: Office Phone:

E-mail: Birthday:

Name:

Address, City, State, Zip:

Home Phone: Office Phone:

E-mail: Birthday:

Name:

Address, City, State, Zip:

Home Phone: Office Phone:

E-mail: Birthday:

Name:

Address, City, State, Zip:

Home Phone: Office Phone:

E-mail: Birthday:

Name:

Address, City, State, Zip:

Home Phone: **Office Phone:**

E-mail: **Birthday:**

Name:

Address, City, State, Zip:

Home Phone: **Office Phone:**

E-mail: **Birthday:**

Name:

Address, City, State, Zip:

Home Phone: **Office Phone:**

E-mail: **Birthday:**

Name:

Address, City, State, Zip:

Home Phone: **Office Phone:**

E-mail: **Birthday:**

Name:

Address, City, State, Zip:

Home Phone: **Office Phone:**

E-mail: **Birthday:**

Name:

Address, City, State, Zip:

Home Phone: **Office Phone:**

E-mail: **Birthday:**

Name:

Address, City, State, Zip:

Home Phone: Office Phone:

E-mail: Birthday:

Name:

Address, City, State, Zip:

Home Phone: Office Phone:

E-mail: Birthday:

Name:

Address, City, State, Zip:

Home Phone: Office Phone:

E-mail: Birthday:

Name:

Address, City, State, Zip:

Home Phone: Office Phone:

E-mail: Birthday:

Name:

Address, City, State, Zip:

Home Phone: Office Phone:

E-mail: Birthday:

Name:

Address, City, State, Zip:

Home Phone: Office Phone:

E-mail: Birthday:

Name:

Address, City, State, Zip:

Home Phone: Office Phone:

E-mail: Birthday:

Name:

Address, City, State, Zip:

Home Phone: Office Phone:

E-mail: Birthday:

Name:

Address, City, State, Zip:

Home Phone: Office Phone:

E-mail: Birthday:

Name:

Address, City, State, Zip:

Home Phone: Office Phone:

E-mail: Birthday:

Name:

Address, City, State, Zip:

Home Phone: Office Phone:

E-mail: Birthday:

Name:

Address, City, State, Zip:

Home Phone: Office Phone:

E-mail: Birthday:

Name:

Address, City, State, Zip:

Home Phone: Office Phone:

E-mail: Birthday:

Name:

Address, City, State, Zip:

Home Phone: Office Phone:

E-mail: Birthday:

Name:

Address, City, State, Zip:

Home Phone: Office Phone:

E-mail: Birthday:

Name:

Address, City, State, Zip:

Home Phone: Office Phone:

E-mail: Birthday:

Name:

Address, City, State, Zip:

Home Phone: Office Phone:

E-mail: Birthday:

Name:

Address, City, State, Zip:

Home Phone: Office Phone:

E-mail: Birthday: